A POET'S JOURNAL   DAYS OF 1945-1951

A POET'S JOURNAL

(GEORGE SEFERIS)

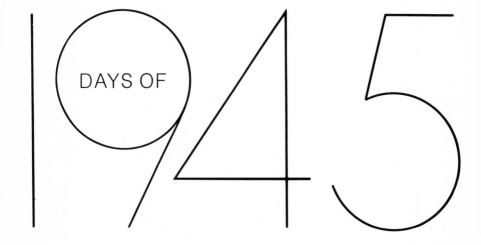

DAYS OF

1945

CAMBRIDGE, MASSACHUSETTS   1974

TRANSLATED BY ATHAN ANAGNOSTOPOULOS

THE BELKNAP PRESS OF HARVARD UNIVERSITY PRESS

ACKNOWLEDGMENTS

For encouragement and assistance in preparing this translation, I am
greatly indebted to many people. I owe special thanks to Mrs. Maró
Seferiadis and to Professors George Savidis, Costas M. Proussis,
Walter Kaiser, and Cedric H. Whitman.

A.A.

Cambridge, Massachusetts
February 1974

CONTENTS

INTRODUCTION   by Walter Kaiser

In 1967, George Seferis decided that the time had finally come to publish
at least this portion of his journals. As he was preparing his manuscript
for the printer, however, the political climate in Greece became increasingly unpropitious for such an undertaking. Soon he did not feel free to
publish in his own country, and in those ominous days there were even
some fears for the safety of his unpublished manuscripts. Accordingly,
shortly before his death on September 20, 1971, he entrusted a copy of
this journal to his friend Athan Anagnostopoulos with the request that he
translate it, that the Harvard University Press publish it, and that I write
an introduction for his American and English readers. All of us who have
been involved in the appearance of this book have felt deeply honored
by this assignment, and the publication of this translation represents an
act of personal homage on the part of each of us to one of this century's

greatest poets and most civilized men. We grieve that he did not live to see its appearance.

These special circumstances no doubt intensified the emotion with which I first read the copy of this diary brought out of Greece; for up to that moment, only a handful of people had seen these pages. Yet I think no one, under whatever circumstances, can fail to be moved by the intimacy and intensity of these journal entries, which take us so completely into the heart and mind of the poet and his creative act, in a way that few other such documents do. There are other great literary journals in this century—Gide's, Woolf's, Camus's, Pavese's—and there are also collections of letters which help us better to understand an author. But I cannot think of many which expose quite so clearly the naked thought and sensibility out of which poems have grown. Generally, the closest we seem to get to the genesis of literary works is in documents such as the canceled version of The Waste Land. This journal, however, reveals to us the deep inner sources of Seferis' poetic achievement. It possesses that candor of revelation and that rare numinous quality which we associate with James's notebooks and the letters of Keats and Rilke.

The existence of Seferis' journal, which he appears to have kept faithfully at least from the age of twenty-five (and perhaps even earlier, since he expressly claims that he began his first journal at the age of twelve), has been known for some time. Visitors to his home in Athens were often shown the shelf on which the beautifully cared-for volumes of the manuscript were, almost piously, arranged, but only a few very close friends had ever read or had read to them by the poet any of the contents. On two occasions, in 1955 and 1966, Seferis permitted the publication of a few pages from the entries contained in this book—enough to confirm what had long been guessed, that this journal itself would become one of the significant documents of modern Greek literature. In 1965 he published a few pages on T. S. Eliot from a later part of his journal, and a short time after his death a segment anterior to the entries in this book, entitled Manscript '41, was also published in Athens. The section published here, however, remains the most substantial portion of these journals that has yet been made public. Happily, it is now also available to

Seferis' countrymen; for it has at last been possible to publish in Greece the original text, which appeared late last summer.

It is hard to know what resonances, if any, the title of this book will have in the minds of those who read it in English. To Seferis' own title, Days of 1945-1951, the publisher has chosen to prefix the explanation, "A Poet's Journal." While that may perhaps assist the buyer by announcing what this book obviously is, it does not begin to convey the complex of emotions and memory Seferis' original title must touch in the minds of his fellow Greeks. For them, the dates alone will evoke the most painful memories of a time of great national tragedy. But beyond that, his title has literary associations at least as powerful as its historical evocations. With it, Seferis joins hands with, and pays tribute to, the greatest of his predecessors in modern Greek literature, Constantine Cavafy, a number of whose most personal and powerful poems begin with the same title, though of course with different dates. And indeed, if any spirit haunts these pages, it is that of Cavafy—Cavafy the European, Cavafy the Greek, the lonely exile, the skeptical political observer, the chronicler of history, the forger of language, the celebrant of love, the man of memories, the witness and martyr (in his tongue the same word signifies both) of the decline of Greek civilization.

.   .   .

Seferis' journal, or more precisely that portion of it printed here, begins shortly after the liberation of Greece by the Allies at the end of World War II. Those war years of Nazi occupation at home and a frustrated, peripatetic government in exile abroad, when so many dragon's teeth were sown for the future, were for Seferis a time of unrelenting official duties and of anxiety, despair, and longing for his homeland; it was also the period of some of his most moving poems. In October 1944 the Greek government in exile, of which Seferis was a member, gathered at the Italian village of Cava dei Tirreni, some thirty miles north of the ancient Greek ruins of Paestum, to prepare for the final stage of their prolonged homecoming. While there, he wrote the last of his magnificent war poems, "Last Stop," in which he sums up the experience of that war perhaps better than any other poet. The fleet which, like those others in their fabled history, brought the Greeks home finally arrived in Athens on October 18—not accidentally, a Tuesday; for it was on a Tuesday almost five hundred years before that Constantinople had fallen. Tuesdays had, since 1453, been thought by Greeks to be days of ill omen, and in retrospect this deliberately dated return seems only to have confirmed, rather than reversed, that tradition. By December, intense fighting between Greek and Greek had broken out in the streets of Athens, and that bloodshed is still going on as this journal begins on New Year's Day. For the return of the Greek government signaled not the end of conflict but the beginning of what historians now call the "Second Round"—the ensuing years of civil war, political intrigue, governmental chaos, foreign intervention, and unspeakable suffering, the spectre of which still stalks Greece today.

The agony of that time informs all these pages, sometimes explicitly, more often just under the surface. Seferis, as Director of the Office of Information during the Regency that governed Greece for almost two years, was entangled in the problems of government and oppressed by the political infighting of that period. A sense of revulsion and exhaustion hangs over the opening pages of this journal. Ultimately, a referendum ended the Regency of Archbishop Damaskinos and brought King George II back to the throne; and shortly after, in October 1946, two years after his return to Greece, Seferis was finally able to escape from the official life of Athens and take his "first vacation since the summer of '37." He and his wife Maró (affectionately called also Marouli in this diary) went off for two months to a house appropriately named Galini—the Greek word for calm, peacefulness, serenity—on the island of Poros near the coast of Argolis.

It is here on Poros that the first of the three central preoccupations of this journal begins. Seferis seems to have had some intimation of what was about to happen to him. "I am starting," he writes, "on a long, very dark voyage, and I'm deeply wounded by my land." Nursing that wound, thinking to escape everything, he comes to the Galini only to discover that his voyage has brought him to the great poem his whole life had been preparing him for. To the reader who knows that poem, "Thrush," these are pages of endless fascination through which one can chart the gradual emergence of this work which, as Seferis says, sums up all the past years and brings to fulfillment ideas for verses he had for some time been jotting down at random in his journal. One finds those "ideas"— phrases, rhythms, images, thoughts—hidden away in this diary from its earliest pages; many of them eventually take their final form in the "Thrush," others are employed even later in Three Secret Poems. His experience of the Galini, "the house by the sea," which gave him as he later said "for the first time in many years the feeling of a solid building rather than a temporary tent," leads him down Proustian paths to speculate on the houses he has known and lost during his lifetime, and these memories become the genesis of the plangent threnody on houses that forms the opening section of the "Thrush." So too, we see him go off one day for a swim and come upon the sunken wreck which provides his poem with its title and one of its basic images. In the same way, we follow his increasing preoccupation with the light—"the most important thing I've 'discovered' since the time the ship that brought me home entered Greek waters." The presence of the sea and the insistence of the "angelic and black light" become more and more overwhelming for him, until in the end he has to close the shutters of his room to block them out in order to finish his poem. As one follows the daily life and thought this journal records, one watches the elements of Seferis' poem take root and flower; one feels the febrile tension of the poetic process, the moments of illumination, the heavy fatigue of creation, inspiration's "sudden flaring up and dying down like green wood burning"; until finally one experiences the drained sense of relief as the poem is completed on the last day of October. If the name of the house on Poros seems strangely to echo the culminating word of Seferis' first great poem, so too the last experience he records on the island echoes an image and a hope expressed in that same poem, "Mythistorema," over a decade earlier. For as he leaves Poros at the beginning of December, the sight of the first almond tree in flower performs a kind of benediction on these weeks of introspection and creativity.

The second great preoccupation or theme of this journal is Cavafy, to whom Seferis' thoughts return again and again. This should not of course be surprising, since Cavafy's achievement can never be far distant from the thoughts of any modern Greek poet; it is something that everyone who would fashion poems in that language must somehow come to terms with. Apparently Seferis' wartime journey in May 1941 to Egypt, whose flat, arid landscape has often suggested insights to admirers of Cavafy, led him to contemplate writing an entire book on this central figure in Greek letters. Impatient with all the "literature" written about Cavafy, he began to make notes toward such a book the following winter in Pretoria, but his wartime duties allowed him little time to pursue such an extended labor. During his vacation on Poros in 1946, though, at the same time he was composing the "Thrush," he returned to his meditations on Cavafy. When he came back to Athens, he brought with him not only his poem but also an essay comparing Cavafy to T. S. Eliot, which he read at the British Council on December 17, 1946, and subsequently published. This important essay, which should now be read in conjunction with this journal, was only an oblique approach to the things he wanted to say, however, and once again, in September 1949, he took up his plans for a full critical study. Yet the subject was only to prove increasingly refractory for him. In some very basic way, his experience of life obliged him ultimately to reject the great art of Cavafy in favor of the humbler, earthy, analphabetic, vital prose of Makriyannis. But one should recognize that such a rejection, if that is even the proper word for it, comes paradoxically only at the ultimate stage of admiration. Concluding, with what sense of loss one can imagine, that Cavafy "in times of stress is not strong enough to help," Seferis finally abandons his plans for a book the following January. Nonetheless, in April 1950 he copies into this journal some of the extensive notes he had assembled the preceding four years in Poros, Athens, and Ankara. Fragmentary and undeveloped though they are, they remain extraordinarily suggestive and provocative, with the insights that only one great poet can have about another. At times they come close to expressing Seferis' own ars poetica. Throughout these critical observations, one is conscious that their special luminosity derives from a lifetime of reading and experience, of asking what it means to be a Greek, of steadfast fidelity to the Muse of poetry.

In February 1948 Seferis was posted to the Greek embassy in Ankara, and the last major section of this journal is written in Turkey, where he spent most of the next three years. His assignment to Turkey represented for him

not merely one more in a long series of foreign posts, but, far more important, his first return to the land of his boyhood. For Seferis had been
born in 1900 in the Greek colony at Smyrna, which was subsequently
forced by the Turks into such tragic exile during the terrible days of
1922. It is hardly an exaggeration to claim that this destruction of Smyrna
was the determining historical event in Seferis' life: it is this that made him
feel permanently and profoundly heimatlos, this that gives all his poetry
its sense of irredeemable alienation, this that demanded his lifelong search
for his identity as a Greek. Although Ankara on its inland plateau is
physically quite distinct from the Mediterranean Asia Minor he had known,
there he felt at least close to the Ionian coasts of his boyhood, and this
proximity filled him with Odyssean emotions of nóstos, homecoming.
Hence it cannot be coincidental that his chief literary preoccupations
during this period are retrospective. During these years he prepared for
publication the first edition of his collected poems from 1924–1946, and
he also spent a long time going over and putting in order the various notebooks of his journal. "I never imagined," he confesses, "this return to the
diary would be so painful."

In late June and early July of 1950, Seferis drove with a friend westward
from Ankara across Anatolia to revisit, for the first time, the Ionian world
in which he grew up. En route he visited the excavations at the ancient
Labraunda directed by the great Swedish archaeologist Axel Persson.
Seferis felt a special affinity for this cultured scholar, whom he calls
"one of the few left us from the old European tradition," because it was
Persson who, earlier in his career, had carried out the excavations at
Asine, the locale of one of Seferis' most famous poems. From Labraunda,
he traveled north via Kos and the ruins at Ephesus until he came at last
to the little village of Skala, on the coast outside Smyrna, where his
family had lived until 1914. He was to return to Skala once more a few
months later, but, as he foresaw, never again: "I understood how Lot's
wife turned into a pillar of salt when she looked back. . . . I shall not
have the courage to return to Skala. One does not make such trips twice."

The burden of emotion in these final pages is almost intolerable. Returning
to the place of his beginnings, Seferis feels that his life has come full
circle and that all his past is both summed and summoned up. "At every

step, memories stir within me overwhelmingly; a constant, almost night-marish piling up of images; incessant invitations from the dead." He thinks of his scattered family and friends, of his brother who had just died and to whom this journal is dedicated, and of a whole civilization that, as he says in one of his poems, had been snuffed out like a small lamp. "Now it is common to speak about the catastrophe of war. How-ever, something that weighs heavier in your guts is the sudden extermina-tion of a fully alive world, with its lights, with its shadows, with its rituals of joy and sorrow, with the tightly woven net of its life." As he wanders among houses fallen into rust and decay or sits in the forever empty ruins of ancient theaters, he contemplates once more the tragedy of Greece, which is the underlying theme of all his work. As a younger man at the ruins of Asine, Seferis had tried to find among the broken bits of stone some living touch of the Greek past. Here, on these shores of suffering, loss, and nostalgia, he searches for fragments of his own past life; and the question he had so movingly asked in "The King of Asine" takes on a fuller and even more personal resonance:

And the poet lingers looking at the stones asking himself
Do they really exist
Among these ruined lines, the edges the points the hollows the curves
Do they really exist
Here where you encounter the passage of rain wind and ruin
Do they exist, the movement of the face the shape of the love
Of those who have so strangely diminished in our life
Of those who have remained shadows of waves and thoughts with the
    vastness of the sea
Or perhaps no, nothing is left but the burden
The nostalgia for the burden of a living existence . . .

"Memory," he wrote in one of the two beautiful poems he composed during his visit to Skala, "wherever you touch it, hurts."

.   .   .

But Memory, as Greeks have always known, is also the Mother of the Muses. Out of the experiences so vividly recorded in this journal, the repository of memory, some of Seferis' finest poetry was created. The chronology of events and experiences I have tried to outline here is, in the last analysis, unimportant. "I didn't have in mind," Seferis explains, " 'to write the story of my life, day by day.' Day by day we live our life; we don't write it." What matters is rather the unique sensibility which shines out of every page. Often Seferis' perceptions have the painful sensitivity of an open wound, "pulsing in the midst of life," and there are entries here written in blood. Often his perceptions are given instantaneous form and shape by his intense mythopoeic awareness, and there are moments when we behold the raw stuff of life miraculously transmuted in the alembic of his poetic imagination. Often his perceptions are endowed with lengthening shadows in the receding perspective of memory. But always, his mind and heart are open to receive whatever life proffers, however rewarding, however painful. And courage is not the least of the qualities that make these pages so memorable.

This journal, in which Seferis persisted all his life, was, he deprecatingly asserts, "written only to keep the habit of the pen." Although he considered it only "second- or third-rate work," he was nonetheless unable to dismiss it, because it held within its pages so much of his life—"not always the most important" things, but those that happened along the way: the death of a cat, the gift of a shepherd's flute, the fragile blossoms of the first cyclamen, the glitter of sun on sea. As he contemplated its eventual publication, he thought of it as his private bouteille à la mer which, he hoped, "may help other seafarers like me." Like all the most significant journals, it tells us not so much what its author did day by day as who he was and who he became as those days went by. It bestows on us, ultimately, the gift of himself, preserving for all time the lineaments of the living, experiencing man and his singular honesty in facing the light of day. As such, these daily jottings are precisely what he so touchingly called them: "the footprints one leaves behind as he passes."

τύμβος ἔχει καὶ γῆς ὀλίγον μέρος· ἀλλ᾽ ὁ περισσὸς
αἰὼν ἀθανάτοις δέρκεται ἐν σελίσιν.

St. Barthélemy
January 1974

IN MEMORY OF MY BROTHER ANGELOS

Today, the 19th of January 1967,
seventeen years have passed.

G.S.

AUTHOR'S NOTE

The pages that follow have stood out, I would say, almost by themselves, among the many that we use to help our memory in various ways. For the time being they are the last of a series, marked by the changes and unavoidable interruptions of current life that must have started in 1925. They refer, needless to add, to the man only and not to his particular professional occupations; to be more explicit, I have not touched the private notebooks of my public life at all. Those are matters for other times—unless they are thrown into the fire in the meanwhile.

As for the names of contemporary persons referred to, one word more. In the first typescript of these pages no one was mentioned by name. I felt that the names would give a personal tone that I didn't want and, in their place, put ellipsis marks. However, two or three friends who read it (I thank them for their careful suggestions) were bothered by those marks. So I decided to use, wherever necessary, fictitious names. I have borrowed them from the streets of Athens; they all have at least the advantage of being, by definition, glorious.

G.S.

Athens
January 1967

1945

NEW YEAR'S DAY 1945. 9 KYDATHENAION STREET

I think: no year like the one that has just passed; nothing more horrible than the last two months.

FRIDAY, JANUARY 12

When you can't write down your whole feeling and your whole thought, everything soon becomes tedious. What's left to us as a whole?

All these days the wretched monotony of cruelty, the sadistic spite of destruction. Yesterday I made the rounds of the wounded city: Athenas, Piraeus, September Third, St. Constantine streets, Kanningos Square. Ruins, ruins; houses blown up, shattered, in that eerie and dreadful humor man's works assume when they're broken up and made useless. Houses cracked open like walnuts, exposing from within vestiges of life that sought to be protected, to create a personal atmosphere. In Promponas' display window (Piraeus St., the shop for hernia trusses), a life-size mannequin behind the broken panes, naked, with a brassiere and a hernia truss. One bullet has pierced her right breast, another the thigh below the corset.

They tell me—Sikelianos: "And I thought the Greeks were a mature people!" Kazantzakis: "Are they perhaps overmature?"

I feel an emptiness when I hear about such talk.

Today the newspapers published yesterday's truce between Scobie and ELAS.*

JANUARY

Postscript to "Gymnopaedia"

The sea that took you away,
soft as a mother's breast,
she knows it.

The questions you asked as a child
are what old men mutter now;
fantasies of useless objects,
like the locked chests of drowned seamen.
Look, they fear the light of the sun;
they fear to see;
they ramble; they have nothing else left.

Children, they grew up starving,
uprooting trees, ravaging mountains;
other children ask and tell you
why they went one step farther—

*General Ronald McKenzie Scobie (1893–), commander of the British forces in Greece, concluded the truce with the communist leaders of ELAS (Greek Popular Liberation Army) that ended the fierce fighting that had broken out in Athens on December 3, 1944.

uphill? downhill?
I don't know; it doesn't matter;
and they have many fires ahead of them
to kindle for the feast of St. John.

I said once, blood
brings blood and more blood—
they thought it a mountebanks' act,
old fairy tales.
Still I whispered, heavy the stones
and immovable the millstones
you heard one night stopping
at the edge of time,
and tragic the young bodies that sank—

"Worn out clothes," said the villains;
but how shall we dress ourselves in the cold
when we have no new ones?
And what can you tell your friends
who grieve and are silent,
while the passionate songs are enjoyed
only by the great whores?

And this still, to discern
a moment of life, to discern
the wind that shakes the roses,
and the roses in the small garden,
five yards of soil, a handful of earth—
I tried this too, I would say,
not at all as a kind of thinking
but as a kind of breath,
my own, your own,
or, rather, as a kind of voice;
the voice is wind and passes.

The sea that took you away
and returned you to the familiar harbor,

offering you
the seven-lighted silence
before the eternal ladder of noon,
knows how to explain
Good Friday and Easter.

SATURDAY, APRIL 7

The real, the palpable, the frightful feeling that reason cannot affect
anyone, that reason is irrational.

In the evening at Xynos' house with Polemon and Spintharos. Both sunk
in black pessimism. "It isn't the Government that's to blame; the whole
country is sick from despair and fear." Conclusion: escape is the only
solution. That's how these political brains talk. Greece today is like
a sick person, condemned by the doctors, abandoned to God's mercy.

MONDAY, ST. GEORGE'S DAY

I've made up my mind to do whatever I can to end this situation that
has lasted now for seven years, the condition to which I have felt bound,
obligated by the war. I did what I could, gave my very best in order to
help. To keep on, I would have to enter politics actively, and I don't want
that. I'll keep working for the only thing that I myself can do, that
depends on me. All those days that went by (one month) I had to make a
great effort to rid myself of the ropes which had cut into my flesh; a
painful effort; I'm just beginning. Since yesterday I've felt better. And
today. God help me.

I've looked over my manuscripts on Cavafy these days. I recalled my
humble and persistent efforts to start writing again in the Transvaal.

Last night Leroa was here. This young man is amazing at times. He read
the essay he wrote as a foreword to his translations. Writing with a
concern almost solely for the harmony of the phrase, not the correct
rendering. He frets unbelievably when you point out an inaccuracy; he

doesn't feel any obligation to correct it. He says "What a pity; the rhythm was much better the other way."

MONDAY, APRIL 30

All these, all these troubles of ours—immutable, unbearable, whatever you want. However, when I go out into the light, when I don't see people, I'm in a state of drunkenness, I feel something deep down in my guts from this land: I'm a foolish vagabond.

MAY 4, GOOD FRIDAY

Last night at the reading of the Twelve Gospels.* Faces in the congregation. When they bring out the crucifix and set it up, they hang garlands of paper flowers and an electric bulb, dark blue like the lights of blacked-out streets in wartime, ugly. But even this, after a while, doesn't bother me; it passes, along with everything else in life.

MAY 6, EASTER

In the nearby taverna they are singing, among other songs, "Christ Has Risen." All thirsting for this Resurrection.

As though I moored today at the harbor that I left four years ago, on Good Friday, at a seaside chapel at Oropos. Relieved and somewhat, sufficiently maybe, lost; like the sailor returning home. Now I use the nights, until 3–3:30 in the morning. The only way to carry out my "release."

I've picked up Cavafy again, very perfunctorily, just to start somewhere. It's difficult; the past seven years weigh on me, and will keep weighing on me for some time to come.

*The twelve passages from different parts of the Gospels, describing the Passion of Jesus Christ, read by the priest during the evening services on Maundy Thursday.

TUESDAY, MAY 8

19:30. The day is ending. Birds are chirping outside in the garden, and my eternal companion, the rooster. I return from the Ministry; time wasted in empty talk. But participation in such talk is part of a public servant's conscientiousness. Today is the day the war ended. In the morning, from the terrace of the Ministry, the parade: evzones who now have turned into mechanical stage sets, puppets wound up to perfection. I have no feeling; the only thing that moved me this morning, looking at the street from the window of my house: a blind man playing the national anthem on his harmonica as he walked along, dragging his feet.

THURSDAY, MAY 24

At the Regency; my "release" a futile dream.

SUNDAY, JUNE 3

Again the daily cares; my new post is not easy. And, what's more, as if things weren't bad enough, Father is coming back with his wife and we must vacate the house; we're moving downstairs, to the first floor. I've moved so many times in my life that the very thought of it leaves me breathless. The trouble is that all the exhaustion of the last few years has surfaced now. It's hard for me to gain a foothold to resist. My God!

JUNE 13

Guile, deceit, and bile for so many years.

SUNDAY, JULY

Today, since morning, at St. Merkourios. My first time since returning to Attica, thus: air of the mountain, breath of pine, curtains of the mountains of Euboea.

Just as when climbing a hillside thick with pine you suddenly see a strip

of burned trees hanging from the sky like fishbones in midair, so too is
the land . . .

As the pines on a hillside take the wind's shape
though the wind has passed, the gust gave the form.
So man's thirst has shaped the words
though man is no longer there—

Yesterday, at —— I hear again the story so characteristic of our times;
Menaichmos reads my Essays;* he's enthusiastic, writes a favorable
review, and brings it to the magazine. Sophroniskos, who is the editor,
tells him: "Your review cannot be published because Seferis is not one of
us." Menaichmos, who had fought in the mountains alongside the guerrillas,
leaves in a rage, wondering what sort of freedom he had fought for.

Yesterday a gathering so the Athenian friends could meet Mr. Symmachidis; speeches. A swarthy young lady read a greeting: heroism, grandeurs
of the resistance, etc. Reply of Mr. S.: heroism, sacrifices, building of a
new world. Emotion in the audience. As they applaud, someone bends
over and whispers in my ear: "Do you know who the young lady is who
was speaking? Tsironikos' former private secretary, from many points
of view, both she and her mother."

SUNDAY, AUGUST 12

Change of emotional horizon.

AUGUST 15, TENOS

Wreaths for the sunken Helle.†

A statue polished by the waves on a shore
and multicolored seashells aflame,

*George Seferis, Dokimes, 2nd ed. (Athens, 1962).
†The light cruiser of the Greek Navy torpedoed in the harbor of Tenos by an
Italian submarine on the Feast of the Dormition of the Virgin, August 15, 1940.

while the chandeliers sway above
and the procession approaches the Great Door.*

WEDNESDAY, AUGUST 28

Colorless, bodiless,
this love advances,
scattered, gathered,
scattered again and again,
yet throbs and beats
in the biting of the apple,
in the bursting of the fig,
into a dark red cherry,
into a rose-colored grape;
so airy an Aphrodite
will thirst, will offer
one mouth and another mouth,
colorless, bodiless

THURSDAY, SEPTEMBER 6

Flying to England. I think of Odysseus, who struggled for ten years to
return to Ithaca from Troy, and I find very insipid the downhill path
we've taken. We diminish, we diminish the earth till we reduce it to a
hazelnut. It's natural to toss it in the end into the infinite void. The
atomic bomb is the natural consequence, etc., etc.

Evening, London. Greek House. Cold. The toilet seat is made of mahogany;
I'd never before sat on such an official throne.

SUNDAY, SEPTEMBER 9, CANTERBURY

I slept in a garret room of the archdiocese of today's successor to Thomas
à Becket.

*The central part of the iconostasis—also called the Royal Door or the Beautiful
Door—is the main entrance into the Sanctuary; only the clergy may enter through it
at definite moments of the divine liturgy.

In the morning to church. This ceremony is interesting. Kneeling priests in the inner depths of the building; colors like the miniatures in a medieval manuscript.

"In thy heart and wounded side" (Hymn 182)

In the afternoon Frank and I went walking in the streets: the "women of Canterbury." The monotony of provincial English towns. I think some-times that the only thing that makes the English different from us (thought, expression, architecture, language) is the light.

"Sufficient for the day is the evil thereof."

SUNDAY, SEPTEMBER 16, LONDON

First quiet day in weeks. I went to see Henry V at the movies.

SATURDAY, SEPTEMBER 22

Flying from Paris to Athens. As I look at it from up here, the rocky nakedness of the Greek land amidst the softness of the sea has in it something terrifying.

SUNDAY, SEPTEMBER 23

Terrible need to sleep and stop seeing people.

SUNDAY, SEPTEMBER 30

At noon to Vouliagmeni with Maró. It's my second swim this summer. On the sand I felt this metamorphosis: a mouse becoming a man again.

WEDNESDAY, OCTOBER 31

Late at night returning home, as I was putting the key in the door, a group of about ten young men (they didn't see me) started singing together: "On the secret seashore . . ." Entering, the telephone again.

SATURDAY, DECEMBER 1

The sun, a pure joy. I phoned Agathias and Charidemos. We walked as far
as Lykovrysi. Everything—mountains, trees, colors, animals—was dancing
with unimaginable delight. On the grounds at Lykovrysi ducks and
rabbits, their bodies so alive.

SUNDAY, DECEMBER 2

I stayed in all day long, arranging papers. Need for this rest.

THURSDAY, DECEMBER 6

How vividly they return, with the mood of the season, images from the
horrible war in Athens a year ago. I'd rather be dead than see such days
again.

Yesterday at the theater. But these people, these emotions, don't belong
only to the author; they belong to me, to the man beside me, to so many,
many others. They are our friends, our brothers who were killed. And
I ask myself what of his own does he bring us, what does he add to this
common nightmare, to this common domain? What uplifting? What
catharsis? He created a lithograph in dull colors that one would prefer not
to look at, that simply irritates.

FRIDAY, DECEMBER 7

At noon on the American warship Providence. I started out glad that I
was going to see a ship. As soon as I went aboard I felt like a captive
in the hands of doctors and nurses preparing to operate. At the stern they
showed us the catapults for the planes. "Like a cannon," explained the
admiral, "they launch the plane at an initial speed of sixty miles per
hour." "And the pilot's head?" someone asked. "It would get crushed of
course," said the admiral very casually, "but there is a special apparatus."
Later they opened the hold where the storageroom and workshop are.
Leaning down, you can see various shining objects in perfect order. A
chamber of scientific destruction. I descended to the launch with relief.

TUESDAY, DECEMBER 11

To breathe. The pressure of these people, unimaginable. In the morning
the following dream: I was in a room with two windows facing the sea.
The house seemed rickety thin, as if made of paper. As if I were inside
a stage set painted very naively. Confused actions and objects. Stanhope is
very jovial, perhaps erotic. Behind the front room another with a round
table and in the background a buffet. It's all familiar; perhaps from the
house at Skala. I sit at the table and open a book; I flip through its pages,
perhaps a book on painting, perhaps a family album. Stanhope sits beside
me; he also looks on with tenderness. Suddenly the ghost of his former
wife appears, with a gray veil, like the young woman in Blithe Spirit,
which I saw in Cairo. I know it's she, but the face doesn't look much like
hers. Her lipstick faded, visibly peeling just as paint peels off when you
burn it. Taxila, tormented, angry, says "When you shut me up there,
in that brothel, I ate pounds and pounds of Arab flesh . . ." In the dream
the intense sensation of the burden of endless intercourse. A crowd of
Arabs appears, fezes and galabias, shouting and gesturing horribly, with
grabbing movements of hands. Then I woke up.

THURSDAY, DECEMBER 13

Yesterday at Tsarouhis' house. His bedroom is also his studio. How does he
work there? We discuss the frontispiece of Log Book II which he is
making. Now he has painted actors, but he has enclosed them in a shack.
The question is how to bring them out of it, into the desert of the Middle
East.

As we were getting up to leave he showed us two pictures of Theophilos,
in one dressed like Alexander the Great, in the other like an evzone.
Unimaginable the tragedy (and the seriousness) painted on this face.
Since yesterday overwhelmed by this impression. I woke up with the
desire to write a poem about Theophilos.*

*Theophilos Hadjimichael (1873-1934), the famous primitive painter from the island
of Mytilene.

Today I wore glasses (for the first time). I feel a bit like a scuba diver.

SATURDAY, DECEMBER

Theophilos' photograph: Caliban loaded with seaweed, etc., emerging from other times. A face like Alexander the Great's, exhausted by his conversation with the mermaid. An Alexander scaly with seashells, carrying the shield of a Negro. Tsarouhis said his costumes were taken from costumes of Italian operas and patched up by himself.

Theophilos

Sleep is heavy on December mornings,
black like the waters of Acheron, without dreams,
without memory, without even a small laurel leaf.
Wakefulness carves oblivion like scourged skin
and the wandering soul rises, holding
shreds of chthonic paintings, a dancing girl
with useless castanets, with legs that stagger,
heels bruised from the heavy tramping of feet
in the submerged gathering below.

Sleep is heavy on December mornings.
And one December worse than another.
One year Parga, another Syracuse,
bones of ancestors unearthed, quarries
filled with crippled men, without breath,
and the bought blood and the sold blood
and the blood divided like Oedipus' children
and Oedipus' children dead.

Empty roads, pockmarked faces of houses,
iconolaters and iconoclasts slaying each other all night long.
Shutters bolted. In the room
the faint light vanishes in the corners
like the blind dove—

FRIDAY, DECEMBER 21

The infants seek to clutch the sun's cobweb in the gardens as their
mothers lift them up.

Tired in the evening, I leaf through the first two volumes of Verlaine.
For years I haven't opened them. I skim through pages at random. With
the exception of a few small poems from the early period, it's impossible
to read beyond the first four or five verses. Boredom brings me to a halt;
it hurts as though I had lost an old friend. Then I read in one breath
the "Après-midi d'un faune" that restores my balance.

CHRISTMAS, '45

Maró is sick. Money troubles. About noon I went out toward Anaphiotika.*
I try to stay down below, to avoid the antiquities. This grace of the
frail, the unsolid, which you see in Greece; a broken-down lintel in three
small pieces is indeed something! It is the light. The most worthless
playthings leap and dance in the light; you watch it transforming them,
turning them into other things, unstable, having no connection with this
misery. Greece is merciless.

I was descending toward the old agora; a couple was going uphill. The
man tall, still young, and cross-eyed; the woman following five or six
steps behind; he was so cross-eyed that while he was talking to her I
thought he was talking to me: "What can we do since they gave us
the wrong key? Was it our fault?"

A Cavafian thought.

Talking with Ktesivios about "Solon's Apologue,"† I wondered how a

*The picturesque quarter of Athens, at the northeastern foot of the Acropolis,
built by the workmen who settled in Athens in the middle 1830's from Anaphi, one
of the Cycladic islands.
†A poem by Angelos Sikelianos, Lyrikos Vios, ed. G. P. Savidis (Athens, 1968),
V, 155–159.

poem could end with the line: "As though it were somebody else's." Can it be that someone else's wisdom is being indiscriminately squandered? "It is perhaps an image referring to the squandering of other peoples' fortunes," he observed very seriously.

1946

FRIDAY, JANUARY 4

Alexander the Great: Your face is familiar. What's your name?
Karaghiozis: Karaghiozis. And you, who are you?
Alexander the Great: Alexander the Macedonian.
Karaghiozis: Ah-hah! I hardly knew you.

(Spatharis' performance)*

TUESDAY, JANUARY 15

Premiere at the National Theater. Performance devoid of any interest.
Sikelianos, tired face, dark glasses. Days ago we heard that he had been
stricken with illness again, in his eyes this time, and had to remain

*Sotiris Spatharis, the outstanding Greek shadow theater (Karaghiozis) player.

in a dark room. As if a bullet were hitting him from time to time: now his leg, now his hand, now his eye. Once the wound has healed, you see him on his feet again crying out that he's the healthiest man in Greece. I hurried over to him and asked after his health. "I worked hard this time and I tired my eyes out. I also had an embolism in the center of my brain. Something that interested me very much."

I was glad he spoke with such courage and I held him by both arms.

"But of course, my friend, just think, to have a ruby in the middle of your brain . . . "

The bell for the curtain rang; we separated. In the intermission he said to me: "I saw you liked what I told you; I'll tell you another story too. Have you ever read Rocambole?*

"I think so, when I was very small."

"It's not possible; you would remember it; it's an important book. Once Rocambole's enemies threw acid in his face. But Rocambole could not be disfigured. Well, his best pupil took him to a famous doctor. The doctor examined Rocambole and told him that in order to restore his face he had to sacrifice his eyes. Rocambole couldn't decide and remained silent. Then from the ajoining room came the voice of the waiting pupil: "Rocambole doesn't need his eyes!"

If Sikelianos were to die, we certainly would be poorer in Greece. Less than a year ago he told me: "I'm in my third youth, Herakles' youth!"

THURSDAY, JANUARY 18

Each new acquaintance is a new worry.

You want to turn into a color or a tree or a marble around which the sky dances. Like the round stone . . .

*The incredible and adventurous hero in a series of popular novels by Pierre Alexis Ponson du Terrail (1829–1871).

And the heart cracked in waiting
And blood sweetly watered the apples—

At Xenagoras', to see the works of Theophilos which he has at his home.
Most of them from the thirties, the period Eleftheriadis had the painter
working almost exclusively in his employ. Theophilos' world: aqueduct in
Smyrna; landscape in Constantinople (lake, church on the left, and river
with ducks in the foreground); Odysseus Androutsos—circular motion
that shows the yataghan; Athanasios Diakos; a Mytilenean; "Greek Dancing
Girl"—the sensation of touching the woman's body—recalls Kalvos' line
"their naked white breasts"; an interior at Easter with two little children
cracking eggs (beautiful painting, a detail hanging on the wall of the
room) and a woman with rolled-up sleeves suckling a baby. Xenagoras
remarks that the baby is not really an infant, but a man. And, indeed,
I see that the baby's face is much more aged than the smooth, expressionless face of the mother. The breast has the wrung out shape of an alembic;
you can't tell whether it's a breast or a nursing bottle. I'm very impressed
with the water's transparency, as well as with his plants. He has a tree,
seen, one would say, from the inside, branches and white trunk and
foliage falling back, looking like the cross-section of an organ of the
human body: kidney, testicles, or heart. In other "portraits" the landscape
is more alive than the person pictured; you think it's going to stride out
of the frame to come and stand beside you to let you see the empty
horizon. Other figures of Theophilos' are sown, made of the same stuff
as the hills and the plants; their flesh is live earth. Some of his plants are
making love or waiting to make love.

In painting, Theophilos seeks to create a human figure, a scene from
everyday life, a landscape; he seeks to represent a theme. But the marvel
is that whatever he has within himself, in his subconscious—tradition,
sensations, repressed desires—emerges to the surface and becomes the
object. He's the bird-catcher, his theme is his lime-twigs. As with every
worthy artist, he has no other meaning. He's a man who has within
himself a broad, collective ego. It is not enough to say that his flowers
remind you of embroideries. Thousands of hands are there, all together,
embroidering from generation to generation. Even the desires that

accompany the girl's embroidery are there, I would say if I were not afraid of mingling literature with his painting.

Thus, from the manner of the hand that creates or the flower that someone cut to speak the language of love or the body that is touched only by dark desire or the ornament that is not abstract but the vessel of a heroic act, the body of a brave youth, e.g., I would seek to find what really moves us in Theophilos.

TUESDAY, JANUARY 22

And two lovebirds holding thistles,
riding wild mastiffs, played and laughed
as the slender reeds bent—

SATURDAY, FEBRUARY 23

Today I finished the lecture on "Erotokritos." Never have I so labored, never so despaired trying to write. I started in the middle of January. There were moments when I felt that my mind had stopped. Hours on end at the table without being able to finish a phrase. At times such frustration that I would get up at night, sit at my desk, and lie down again utterly exhausted, leaving innumerable torn-up sheets of paper. In the end the lecture was written in four days when I was able to shut myself up at home without going to the office and without answering the telephone. The truth is that my acquaintance with the poem since the time of my youth helped me.

MONDAY, MARCH 11

I spoke at 7 at Parnassos. People listened almost hypnotized. When I had finished, a long interval elapsed before they realized that I was no longer speaking.

MONDAY, MARCH 25

National holiday. Parade before the Unknown Soldier. The English
Ambassador holds an umbrella for rain, pure decoration. I'm almost
moved to tears by the disabled veterans and little children.

FRIDAY, APRIL 5

First summer day.

Though April has come with palms and lilacs,
I hear nothing now, as though it had snowed all night.

APRIL 21, EASTER

At Psychiko until sunset; certainly Psychiko is the most stupid landscape
in Attica.

In the afternoon George Apostolidis; I saw him for the first time yesterday; he had just returned from Switzerland after so many difficult years—
for both of us.

SATURDAY, APRIL 27

Yesterday at Gelon's. We talk about Sikelianos. When they drew blood
from him he said he liked his own blood. He's now writing The Death of
Digenis and says that the end of the work will coincide with his own.
Sikelianos plays with death and is amused by it. Even here, he's beyond
the usual wretchedness of men.

SUNDAY, APRIL 28

In the morning to an official movie. Athletic demonstrations at Moscow's
Red Square last August. They bring to mind Hitler's celebrations with
flags and organized masses or a colossal American music hall.

In the afternoon to Phaneromeni where Sikelianos is spending his Easter holidays.* Pyrgotelis had phoned me last Monday that Sikelianos had been stricken again, that they had given him up. Gelon here too. I set out with a heavy heart. The crossing from Pefko by boat reminded me of chthonic voyages. And yet infinite beauty. Infinite in the literal sense. Phaneromeni is now a nunnery, shining with cleanliness and whitewash. Anne was cheerful, Angelos playful. Completely well, if one can say that. We descended. The sun was combing the green grass with a golden comb. Odor of chamomile. "How beautiful it is," he said in a soft voice, almost whispering. I remember only this.

TUESDAY, APRIL 30

Yesterday the last meeting of the Executive Board of Directors of the National Theater, to which I belong. The president is Loukas Kanakaris-Roufos. In the morning, citations to the Hellenikon Haima. "The National Theater is restored to Greece. A definitive end has been put to the swarm of EAM—KKE!"†

SUNDAY, MAY 5

To Varkiza with George Apostolidis. My first swim in the sea.

SUNDAY, MAY 12

A second swim, at Vouliagmeni. The unexplained magic of the sea. How quickly it changes me; this is my amazement, deep amazement, in my very bones. I can't understand. I must go nearer, cross this line of separation into another world.

Unimaginable how much patience is needed to see even the simplest things. How much patience I need to write a single verse.

*The poet Angelos Sikelianos (1884–1951).
† The resistance organization National Liberation Front (Ethnikon Apeleftherotikon Metopon) and the Communist Party of Greece (Kommounistikon Komma Ellados).

MONDAY, MAY 20

Reception at the French embassy. Eluard had just arrived. We exchanged only a few words. Face and body tired, as if it would take only a gust of wind to blow him away. This man of about fifty gives the impression of being Gide's grandfather, a septuagenarian when I first met him. All the machinery is ready here to turn him into a political mishmash.

FRIDAY, MAY 24

Eluard's lecture at the French Institute: "Poésie et vérité." It's amazing how much he repeats himself; in his lecture one recognizes whole sections from a lecture he gave in London in 1936 (see "Donner à voir"). The best was when he read his poems. Not that his poems made the impression on me which comes like a sudden illumination or even a sudden thrill, but he certainly has both the feeling for rhythm and the feeling for the word; there's a soft flame in this sickened body. And yet, what a miasma of phoniness surrounds him: one wonders how many of those insanely applauding would have stayed if he were not their political tool. If he weren't theirs, all of them would have found him a decadent artist, indeed, of the most bourgeois degeneracy in precisely these very poems.

The art of decadence, as they call it, is not the outcome of critical thought; it is a slogan for political propaganda.

I noticed this: Eluard never asks questions.

MONDAY, MAY 27

Yesterday, at the Attiko. A full house, an atmosphere of political demonstration. Party leaders are applauded as they enter. Eluard: "La poésie pour tout le monde." As he speaks, many read newspapers; they don't want to waste their time until the moment of the translation. Kazantzakis and Sikelianos each read at the start a greeting to the poet, first in French and then in Greek. But what meaning does this polyglotism have? I find it humiliating. Kazantzakis says: "Now love is armed" (Amour armé). Why "now"? Sikelianos bursts into an exuberant speech. It all makes me sick.

Today Leroa's lecture about Sikelianos at the French Institute with Eluard presiding. While we are waiting to go to Symmachidis' house, I walk with Charidemos in the garden. Suddenly Eluard, all by himself, almost staggering from exhaustion, comes straight toward us asking if there's a seat or bench anywhere. I bring him a chair. Mrs. S. seeing me carrying it says to me, "Oh! Don't take Eluard away from us!" As if I were about to take him to my house. They'll squeeze the poor thing like a lemon. He's a wreck. Tired. Tired. He gazes at the stars with dull eyes: "Five receptions this afternoon," he whispers, "I can't take anymore!" "I wonder how you can stand the life you lead," I said to him.

"The triumph of the literary movement of the Resistance was its refusal to hate" (Horizon, May 1945). Has Eluard perhaps realized that in Greece he has entered the machine of hatred?

He said to Charidemos (who was telling him about the language difficulties a Greek poet encounters): "But why don't you write in French?" "But it isn't my language; I don't know it well enough for writing poems." "But, if you stay a year in Paris, you'll learn it. Anyway, what significance does a language have? I myself could even write in Chinese. That's why I don't admit that a poem can be untranslatable . . . "

Strange; I thought that what characterized him was a very deep and genuine feeling for his language. I felt this when I heard him reading his poems. The rhythm of that voice remained in my ears forty-eight hours. This too is a consequence of his theory "La poésie pour tout le monde." The poet is everybody, poetic language is every language, even one we know badly. "Poetry for everybody" is a theory contradicted by his whole being, exactly as his whole emotional fabric rebels against this political machinery in which he has become entangled. Eluard the man is here, his theories elsewhere; he's crushed between.

WEDNESDAY, MAY 29

Yesterday the last Eluard experiment. After all those manifestations that

had turned him into an amorphous pulp, excursion to Pefko. The two
Sikelianos, the two S's—Anne invited them the last moment (God, save
the poet from his patrons!), Charidemos, Leroa. We started out at 3:30. I
was so downhearted that I took my bathing suit along for a life preserver;
when I threw out the idea, I had imagined very different company.

Daphni, the sea a golden mosaic, and then, without stopping, Pefko.
A boat; I rowed. At the beach at Phaneromeni I left the others to climb
uphill and threw myself into the sea. Eluard no longer interests me, man
to man. I have nothing to do with him beyond social chatter. His political
friends have insulated him like an electric wire. I climbed to the monastery
as the sun was setting one of those eternal May evenings, indestructible.
From within a cloud, opened like the Pantocrator's eye, the sun cast its
rays upon a blue mountain that each moment changed mass, weight,
transparency. I entered the monastery yard, totally empty. Worn out
bas-reliefs built in the plastered wall and bells hanging low like ripening
fruit. Outside, among the others, the poet had changed; that rag, that
machine, had become human. Attic nature had classified each one,
relentlessly as usual. The instructors useless, like old one-horse shays.
He said: "Could I perhaps live, could I end my days in such a land?" The
shipwrecked mask had fallen like a yellow leaf. From now on one could
talk to him. But it's too late now. I wanted, however, to open exactly this
door for him: if he can see, if he can remember.

Since the beginning of spring, an ineffable sensibility and elation. A
swelling of heart and senses; an uncrystallized state, very chaotic; humaneness intensified; a murky frenzy spread everywhere. Impossible to find
word, gesture, or intercourse that can express it. The words, a lump in the
throat. Sensibility burns out without bursting. I go wherever it takes me,
blind.

SUNDAY, JUNE 2

Since morning in the woods of Kineta.

"What we are only God can complete." Impossible to use: they mean nothing, the word "beauty" or the word "nature" when speaking about the face of Attica.

Dialogue between man (myself, o altra cosa) and man (or a god); this incessant exchange with the sea, the mountains, the light, and the air.

The mountains, each inside the other, are bodies hugging each other, flowing into each other; they proceed and complete you. The same with the sea. This amazing thing happens. It is impossible for me to express this revelation in a better way. After this, whether or not you are a person has no significance. Or, the person is no longer you, the person is there. If you can, you complete it. If you can, you perform a sacred act. At this point, happiness or unhappiness mean nothing; it is a struggle that takes place elsewhere.

Diastole of the soul in this other world. A frightful abyss gaping before you to the systole of the soul you experienced when you too were stained by the fraternal killing. How can you cross this abyss?

Unbearable, painful silence.

Dizziness. In this abyss the belly of a woman becoming more and more the belly of an unknown woman, the belly of the earth.

The black and angelic Attic day.

TUESDAY, JUNE 4

He went blindly
into the warm meadow,
and saw darkness
behind the light.

At noon at the archaeological museum. They unearth now—some in crates, some bare to the flesh in the earth—the statues. In one of the big old galleries, familiar from our student years, with the dull facade that somewhat resembled the dreary public library, the workmen excavate with shovels and pickaxes. If you didn't look at the roof, the floor, the windows, and the walls with inscriptions in gold, this could be any excavation site. Statues, still sunken in the earth, appeared naked from the waist up, planted at random. The arm of some colossal god, curved in toward his thigh, extended below the scaffolding; a naked woman who had turned her back to me was bonneted with a worker's gray basket that allowed only her smiling buttocks to show. It was a chorus of the resurrected, a second coming of bodies that gave you a crazy joy. Elsewhere statues lying down, bas-reliefs set up upside down. Emotion from this sudden familiarity. The bronze Zeus, or Poseidon, lying on a crate like an ordinary tired laborer. I touched him on the chest, where the arm joins the shoulder, on the belly, on his hair. It seemed that I touched my own body. I thought I would gladly have given him to enjoy the woman I might have loved. I also thought that the artist who created this body held in his hands the consciousness that he was endowing with life a god who had very often commited adultery among mortals; it seemed strange: this huge man, lying on his back, had the posture of an infant.

Crazy about the land. Every day carried away more and more by this drunkenness. The sea, the mountains that dance motionless; I found them the same in these rippled chitons: water turned into marble around the chests and the sides of headless fragments. I know my whole life won't be long enough to express what I have been trying to say for so many days now: this union of nature with a simple human body, this worthless thing—superman they'd say today. As I'm writing now, I make desperate gestures in the void and express nothing.

And yet I'm crazy about these things, in this light.

"And you see the light of the sun"—

as the ancients used to say. I could analyze this phrase and advance toward the most secret love. But to say what you want to say you must create another language and nourish it for years and years with what you have loved, with what you have lost, with what you will never find again.

For the moment—

Behind us, in the wounded galleries, a young man with a blank face walked for a while, strikingly solemn and withdrawn. The friend accompanying me said: "He's a deaf-mute, but he knows all the European languages; he can even read hieroglyphics." For the moment I'm like him: I know languages, I also know how to read hieroglyphics somewhat. But I am a deaf-mute. It is not easy among these whores and billy goats.

In a gallery, "Cavafian" impressions:

A series of portraits (sculpture): a Sophist, bald, bearded. Some familiar sophist, "leaving for Syria," or another, an Alexandrian cotton merchant, e.g., a little past the middle of the last century. Something between Rothschild and a Greek notable in a large colony: Odessa, Marseilles, Egypt. Alexandrian baroque. Bust of Antinous: "Dreamy eyes, dreamy lips," at the same time unimaginably dead, like the hair of the dead in a locket.

Leroa told me a few days ago: "Really, I'm not lucky. The so-and-so writing (in France Libre, I think) praises my sentence, 'Cavafy has created Hellenism's Arabian Nights tales.' This sentence is not mine, it's yours. Gide, when I was reading him my preface, at the sentence: 'Then, one would say, the journey continued, 'perpendicularly . . . ' observed: 'Ah! ça, vraiment c'est une trouvaille.' That is not my sentence either; it's yours. I'm certainly not lucky.'" "I have no presumption of ownership in these things," I told him. "Anyway, these sentences in your text differ in meaning from mine."

I wasn't just being polite; his candor had moved me. I was not upset. On the contrary, I felt pleased, not because these sentences were liked (borrowed, like other things, from my diary, which I read to him, or my conversations) but because they were liked while I remained unknown.

THURSDAY, JUNE 6

What if this flame is snuffed out? The empty body.

I woke up amidst thorns . . .

And this nameless mermaid, with arms that can entwine like her legs, to embrace the limbs with such ease and persistence, just as a sculptor's hand rends the clay in the throes of birth.

MONDAY, JUNE 17

All these past days a wilting, a sickly condition. Pains in the back, misery, silence. Now again the sinuous womanly torso with the mountains you want so much to touch after you've bathed in the sea and the sun scorches you.

There is a drama of blood played out between the light and the sea, all around us here, that very few sense. It is not sensualism; it is something much deeper than the fleeting desire and the so persistent smell, let's say, of woman that prisoners yearn for. There is a drama of blood much deeper, much more organic (body and soul), which may become apparent to whoever perceives that behind the gray and golden weft of the Attic summer exists a frightful black; that we are all of us the playthings of this black. The stories we read about the houses of Atreids or Labdacids show in some way what I feel. Attic tragedy, the highest poetic image of this hemmed-in world, constantly striving to live and breathe upon this narrow golden strip of land, meanwhile, with little hope of being saved from sinking to the bottom. This creates its humaneness.

But unseen fields snatched him
borne to some invisible
death

(Oedipus at Colonus, II. 1681–1682)

In the Oresteia the same drama of blood ends in the earth's depths. And in that folk tale's land that does not die men do not die but vanish. This end is not the feeling of death; it is the knowledge of the abyss.

Late at night. More difficult to complete a verse than lift a rock.

MONDAY, JUNE 24

By chance rereading St. John Perse's Anabase in Eliot's English translation (London, 1930), I notice:

Tomorrow the festivals and tumults, the avenues
planted with podded trees, and the dustmen at dawn [. . .]
the election of harbour-masters the voices trilling
in the suburbs [. . .] *

I think of Auden's "Spain":

To-morrow the hour of the pageant—master and the musician,
the beautiful roar of the chorus under the dome
to-morrow the exchanging of tips on the breeding of terriers
the eager election of chairmen
By the sudden forest of hands . . . †

WEDNESDAY, JUNE 26

Yesterday afternoon I read Mencius on the Mind. Richards always interests me:

King Sun one day saw an ox which was brought to be sacrificed for the consecration of a bell. The animal was very frightened. King Sun could not bear this expression of fright and ordered them to replace it with

*St.-J. Perse, Anabasis, tr. by T. S. Eliot (London, Faber and Faber, 1930), pp. 35–37.
†W. H. Auden, "Spain 1937," Collected Shorter Poems (London, Faber and Faber, 1937; New York, Random House, Inc.), p. 11.

a sheep (page 67). Not having seen the sheep, he didn't mind their killing it. I'm not absolutely sure if this is hypocrisy.

On page 74 this interests me:

"Adroitness rather than force, persuasion rather than bullying is his recommendation in the management of the wishes. His attitude to himself and to those factions in himself which might challenge his supremacy is markedly different from that which Judaism has given to the West. The Will is for him a Ruler and the Confucian conception of an ideal Ruler is always of one who rules by benevolence, by caring for the interests of the governed, by consent. To take up arms against his subjects is the mark of a bad Ruler, who has not performed his duties and deserves to be deposed. Mencius keeps the conception unchanged in applying it to the will. It is even possible that this way of stating the matter reverses it—that the Confucian conception of the Ruler derives from the Chinese moral attitude to the self, rather than the other way about. There is no officially recognized war in the Chinese mind between the Soul and the Body, between will and desire."*

I'm thinking of the Zen attitude.

SATURDAY, JUNE 29

Incredible need for the countryside, even a tree.

MONDAY, JULY 1

At 00:01 (Athens time) the atomic bomb fell on Bikini. It's name is "Gilda" (the newspapers).

FRIDAY, JULY 12

    Partiality

With eyes that saw
not the body but the veins,

*I. A. Richards, Mencius on the Mind (London, 1932), pp. 74–75.

with veins that touched
not the flesh but the nerves,
with nerves that met
not the lips but the teeth,
with teeth that bit the belly;
with belly that received the horror
not the sperm,
and the horror swelled the breasts
and beggars sucked them;
serene, beautiful, and tender,
she waited for the next day,
the next month, the next year,
among us, ecstatic.

MONDAY, JULY 15

As I'm dressing in the morning, barrel organs play outside in the street.
Marching songs of the "Panathenaia of 1912-1913," tunes of the Balkan
Wars. Signs of the prevailing tomb-looting in today's Greece. They exhume
everything: people, thoughts, feelings, music.

FRIDAY, AUGUST 3

At the Ministry yesterday morning: I seemed to smell the pharmaceutical
emissions of a hospital. It's an intense sensation that grabs me by the
nostrils, as though I'm in some refuge for rare neurotics. Their words,
their nagging, their rages, their reactions—all unfounded. As I was saying
something like this to a friend, he remarked: "All of Greece is like that."
Today, waking, these things come to mind again, while outside the barrel-
organ plays the interminable songs of the "Panathenaia of 1912-1913."
Poor Greece. I begin to think seriously—and the thought is horribly
tormenting—that after the unprecedented concentration of Hellenism on
Greek soil (during interwar years) only the possibility of a new diaspora
would allow the Greeks to accomplish anything. Today one sees clearly the
psychological symptoms of famished shipwrecked men adrift on a stripped

raft. They try to devour each other: Le radeau de la "Méduse."

TUESDAY, AUGUST 6

Days alike and indifferent in the heat. The mind doesn't work, the entire man falls into a deadly state; he moves only by habit.

I've been looking over The Waste Land again these days. I made some corrections, three important ones. I started planning a lecture on Cavafy and Eliot.

Tourmer wants me to help him translate some of my poems. Unbearable. I did something like that, casually correcting, with the help of friends, translations of the young Valaoritis and Bernard Spenser; few things could thrust me into more boredom.

No one will be able to understand what this war has cost me. How difficult my "release" now seems.

Today at Sikelianos' at Kifissia. They kept us for supper. Suddenly Angelos, when they brought in the food, leaped up: "I'm trembling with hunger, I can't suppress my desires any longer."

He tells me confidentially that Kazantzakis wrote him from London to propose to the Nobel Committee that it divide the prize between the two of them. A strange people.

SUNDAY, AUGUST 11, POROS, GALINI*

I finally tore myself away from Athens last Friday on the landing craft Sophades. Slow voyage, terribly hot, but nothing matters since I'm getting away. First time here since Holy Week 1940; first time in the Greek countryside in six years; a landmark. You look back and add it all

*"Serenity," the house by the sea, near the Naval School, which was being used as a hotel.

up. What will I do after the referendum? Chaotic unknown; another turning point in my life. The trouble is that in such circumstances it's good to start out with fresh strength. Unfortunately for me, the exhaustion of the last seven or eight years is finally surfacing.

This voyage is like a return to Greece.

TUESDAY, AUGUST 13

I count the days—when I count them—like a miser. When I think of Athens it's as a nightmare, a noisy nightmare.

Poros isn't my place. Though one of the few Greek countrysides where I've "lived," it is certainly not my place. Anyhow, ten years ago, coming here from Aegina, I called it a whore's bedroom. It has something of Venice—a canal, communication between houses by boat, luxury, languor, sensual temptation (Lemon grove, etc.)—a place for famous lovers of the international set. There's a sort of hemmed-in space here, with many charms to be sure, something of a pit of lustfulness, with the moon overhead and brassy music from the Naval Training Camp all day. Last night, going up to bed, I stood for a moment on the balcony of my room looking at the mountaintops opposite. I remembered the foreign friend who said "for me, the sea is a pit." I thought of this channel's passage out to the cliffs of Hydra and I felt relieved: if I had to leave it would be to return to the dreadful life of Athens. Two winters of good work, even here, would cleanse me of the horror of always feeling like an exile in the world—not among men; I love men—but in this world of repressive sterile attrition.

It's 4:30 in the afternoon and hot. I went down to the dining room after pouring a number of buckets of water over myself. As I was writing, Aglaope passed in her bathing suit, lightfooted as a dancer, coming out of the sea. She said, "I couldn't sleep." Drops of sea-water on her skin.

Yesterday, for the first time since our arrival, late, around eight in the evening, we went shopping in the city with Marouli, who left this morning. I amused myself, as if it weren't me watching the bustle in the port, sailboats and big power boats moored at the pier. One little boat had a badly painted girl right in the middle of the sail. The boatman (an ugly fellow) said, "it's my fiancée"—the stuff of Elytis.* Shops and grocery stores with much atmosphere, with lithographs and other pictures, with unlikely merchandise. One barbershop was called "Eve." Above the face of a customer thick with shaving suds, a picture of Adam, Eve, the snake, the tree, the apple—all the proofs. The attentive, stumpy barber, razor in hand, looked strikingly like the Adam (in the lithograph).

How much rust must I scrape off myself?

WEDNESDAY, AUGUST 14

The village clock is a kind of campanile on top of the rock of Poros. You can see the hour (from the Galini) with binoculars. The houses have the color and luster of white enamel at times—this light.

A walk toward the lighthouse yesterday. Not all the way; we stopped a little beyond the Russian naval station. We passed through camps, sometimes a hotel-like installation under a pine tree: a shiny brass bed, a wash-stand, a chair with a towel hanging over its back—"the walls of my room fell down so I lived in the garden," as Tonio said. The space between the naval station and the beach is fenced in with wire. Who owns that? A little farther there's a hut on a hill. The dog is ferocious. An old woman shouts "Get inside, you devil!" Beneath the hut, a melon field. "You've got a nice melon field, Madam," we said. "It'll get better," she said, "when we bring the water down from up there," pointing to the mountain as if the whole region were hers. Here apparently you can be a landlord if you own a dog and set up a hut somewhere.

Afternoon. The days pass, the days pass. Touti is spread out in front of me on the table.

This morning at the sea. Afterward newspapers, like the sudden ripping of

*The poet Odysseus Elytis (1911–).

bandages from miserable wounds. How can the same man who swam in the water be the one who now reads the newspaper? This I just can't understand.

FRIDAY, AUGUST 16

Tomorrow we leave. Since the day before yesterday the moon has been on the wane. The lagoon of Poros with its lights that I spell out every night, appears to sink deeper each day. Poros, enclosed as it is, nonetheless reminds me how few things I need, that I should dispense with things that prevent me from seeing. What I have here before me is enough: a piece of driftwood on the beach, the brassy sound from the Training Camp, the lithographs in the grocery stores of the town, the blank faces suffice for me to write what I wish. I no longer believe very much in wide horizons.

Amazing survival: as soon as I'm in the country—the habits of childhood. A boatman's chat, a fisherman's gesture have an authenticity for me that I have felt only very rarely in the company of so many ministers or professors or intellectuals. They belong, even today, to a ceremonial world. But the others . . .

At the Galini everything emits an odor of the faded romanticism (in the English sense) of the last quarter of the past century. Most of the books in the library are by forgotten English authors. Boîte à musique bought in Geneva in 1876: lovely inlaid wood, brass cylinder with tiny spikes, little bells, seven or eight tunes—"La sensitive," "Les cloches du monastère," "Faust," "Traviata," "La fille de Madame Angot," etc., written in calligraphy on a piece of cardboard nailed to the cover, with the crest of the kings of Great Britain—"Dieu et mon droit"—and beneath, "Valse, rien ne peut changer mon âme." This box is a small ark which has made time stand still for seventy years now with its seven or eight pieces. "Flacon débouché" is a measure of today's dizziness.

This morning we took the boat and went around to Daskaleio for a swim.

Between the tiny island and the beach lies the sunken <u>Thrush</u>. Only the funnel rises up above the surface a few inches. "They sank her so the Germans wouldn't take her," they told me. We looked down. The gently rippling water and dancing sunlight made the submerged little ship, seen quite clearly with its broken masts, flutter like a flag or a dim image in the mind. The boatman said, "After she sank, the black-marketeers stripped her bare."

AUGUST

At the National Garden: the cicadas like those at Skala. Cape Kapodistrias, Cape Valaoritis.

WEDNESDAY, OCTOBER 2

Leaving the harbor of Piraeus for Poros: a ship with her bow stuck in the bottom and propeller in the air like an iron lily.

Between the knowledge of life and the knowledge of death,
    am I perhaps no more than a feather on top of the wave?

. . . <u>but to the oars</u>! The ship whistles— Πόρος, πόρος, ἄπορος —*

SATURDAY, OCTOBER 5 , POROS, GALINI

I came here last Wednesday, when a long period of my life in service had come to a close—eight or nine years, starting from the period of the Anschluss. The Ministry has given me two months' vacation, my first since the summer of '37. I'm thinking of spending it here or wherever they will leave me in peace. I want to be able to think.

I started out downhearted, in very bad humor. I don't remember such a thing ever happening to me. Before, each time I took off for the country, all my city scales fell from me as soon as I set foot on the ship; I felt free. But now I am not starting out for the country; I am starting on a long,

*Poros, passage, impasse.

very dark voyage, and I'm deeply wounded by my land.
I haven't been in the mood to turn to this notebook these days. All my
dreams (those of sleep) are reenactments of my public life and my
monologues (early in the afternoon today I took a long walk along the
road to the monastery) are filled with utterances of this same kind. I
carry much filth within me that must go.

What I must guard against now is that my life is measured. I no longer
have the almost unlimited horizons one takes for granted when he makes
plans in his youth.

MONDAY, OCTOBER 7

    Notes for a poem (May–June)

Eyelash-curled, gentle-smiling girl,
deep-girdled in tragic calm—

Though I sing amid the skeletons
and souls that burnt the oil,
alone in the deserted courtyard
of a monastery left over from Turkish conquest,
looking at motionless bells that mellow—

With my pencil I drew the secret bed,
and all around flaming brambles licked the limbs,
shadows of snakes coiled about the swarthy loins,
and in the belly's lake a red eel swam—

Sometimes in the moonlight
the statues bend like reeds
amidst the tender fruits and hounds
and the flame becomes a tender oleander—

And the lads who dived from bowsprits

of the caiques, still winding spindles,
naked bodies plunging into the years,
holding a coin in their teeth, still swimming
under water, as the calm smiles
and the light sews with golden stitches
sails and wet wood and sea colors;
even now you see them going slantwise
toward the pebbles of the depths, the white lekythoi.
Do not complain: I do not speak of the past
or of things I wish were different;
I speak of love: both yours and mine—

And you who left the palaestra to take the knives
and you who shot with arrows the resolute marathon runner
who saw the finish drowning in blood
through childhood images,
and the world emptying like the moon,
and gardens withering—

Masked companions dancing
on a mountain peak where destruction trod a while ago,
playing with colored ribbons,
dancing, look at them, the hobbyhorse—

And the sun piercing the foliage
throws golden sequins to the ground
in answer to each offering of ours—

Just as the Doric chiton with the wind's breath
forms curves and ripples on the belly, thighs, and chest
and desire runs through the wrinkles like an eel—

Just as the wrinkled faces of old men
fall like masks into open pits—

When spring returns with nests in her arms and with swallows,
eyelash-curled, deep-girdled, the great embrace—

Love, man's peaceful abode.

(Meng Tzu, 17)*

Those who climbed the steps
and those who fell down the stairs—

The royal eagle ate one grape and another grape
and dug his claws into the sterile belly
and I saw from within the clouds a flame pour forth
vanishing in the blood-stained wave on the seashore.

Antares: the cherry-red dog-tooth of Aphrodite.

Women buying fruit in the summer
in ports of Anatolia, Smyrna, Jaffa, Syracuse,
cities closed like shutters in the afternoon, cool cities!

Sounds of music in closed houses,
sailors on shore and kings of Anatolia with caravans—

Lord, remove the haze from before our eyes; it is lead.
Remove the net of nerves and desire,
dry up the deep river of thirst,
let us see, let us pass.
Our hands are bridges like babies
in their mother's arms in the gardens
where they stretch their palms to caress
the golden tassels of the sun—

Empty seas, empty ships, weak heads,
souls caught in the web of the great spider—

And at dawn you heard a voice howling:

*Richards, Mencius on the Mind, appendix p. 17.

"Remember, Father, the baths where you were slain!"*
Not only in the hive of the treasure-laden graves
but here too in the neighborhoods of all-night movie houses,
in the city's garden swallowed by the night,
at Syntagma, before the Unknown Soldier.
How many moments of silence does a life cost?
"Remember, Father, the baths where you were slain!"
Only blood will water life and the nightingale,
while it sings out its desire behind locked grilles
for little children who will come tomorrow to play with new rattles—

Love mowed down, how the cicadas suddenly stop all at once—

Endless laughter of waves on the highways of the sea.

(Absent-minded, one condemned to death by all
passes in the streets with bent head.)

Small fans of other times
or colors on costumes of actors, dimly remembered,
sometimes shine—

I pass before icons which I destroy;
the great iconostasis—

(Climbing on words like a rope ladder, the poem must proceed by itself
and complete itself. It is not that easy; slowly, very slowly.)

TUESDAY MORNING, OCTOBER 8

I have been working on Cavafy again since last Saturday afternoon. I am
reading articles about the poet written in the past and more recently.
They bore me. Too much "literature," too much padding in all of them;

*Aeschylus, Libation Bearers, l. 491.

very few noteworthy observations. I don't yet know if I'm in Cavafy's ambience. A thought put aside for the moment: I am trying to return to the habit of working.

I'll read every morning—I started yesterday—about a hundred lines of the Iliad.

Yesterday and today were superb days, too much for me; they distract me; I feel terribly lost. As in a ruined house, I have to put many things in order. I don't know if I'll ever be able to reconstruct it.

After swimming: the light is such that it absorbs you as a blotter does ink; it absorbs the personality.

Days are stones. Flintstones
that accidentally found each other and made two or three sparks,
stones on the threshing floor, struck by horseshoes, and crushing many
  people,
pebbles in the water with ephemeral rings,
wet and multicolored little stones at the seashore,
or lekythoi, gravestones that sometimes stop the passerby
or bas-reliefs with the rider who went far out to sea
or Marsyas or Priapus, groups of phallus-bearers.
Days are stones; they crumble one on top of the other.

WEDNESDAY, OCTOBER 9

This hothouse atmosphere of Poros. I need better air. I have no choice: the problem is to find four walls to protect me. Always lost, but now I know these conditions when I return to my work; they do not surprise me. Nor can I rid myself of the anxiety of passing time—a bad habit.

I read through Cavafy taking notes. I don't know at all, not at all, if it's possible now to finish the work I started in Pretoria—like so many others that have been put aside in the sort of life I lead.

Today I was reading Matthew Arnold (the first essay of his I have ever read): "The Choice of Subjects in Poetry." I note: "The terrible old mythic story on which the drama was founded stood, before he entered the theatre, traced in its bare outlines upon the spectator's mind; it stood in his memory, as a group of statuary, faintly seen, at the end of a long and dark vista . . . " (English Critical Essays, XIX Century, The World's Classics, Oxford.)

I said in my preface to Eliot: "When myth was a common feeling the poet had at his disposal a living medium, a ready emotional atmosphere where he could move freely and approach his surrounding fellowmen, where he could express himself . . . "* Sometimes such coincidences amuse me; however, etc.

Anguish of time always.

We moored beneath the trees. Huge eucalyptuses; red and white oleanders among the cypresses along the lane; and grapes on the arbor, clusters of grapes half-eaten by bees; women yellow from fever, carrying babies; and a corner of the cistern, the color of an old mirror struck by the setting sun—

SATURDAY, OCTOBER 12

I read, to start my day, Eliot's Four Quartets. (Actually, compared to them, Cavafy's poetry looks Egyptian; I mean from the outlook of physical geography, the outlook that made an impression upon me when, by the harbor of Port Said, I saw the shores of Egypt for the first time.) I seemed to be reading them for the first time; for the first time I got the impression of this tempo (like Beethoven's Fifteenth Quartet more specifically like the "Canzona di Ringraziamento"). And this too: their theme is Time, just as time is in essence the subject of music. If I had read the following in '35, I would have put it as an epigraph to the Mythistorema:

. . . As we grow older
The world becomes stranger, the pattern more complicated

*T. S. Eliot, I Erimi Chora Kai Alla Poiemata (The Waste Land and Other Poems), introduction, notes, translation by George Seferis (Athens, 1949).

Of dead and living. Not the intense moment
Isolated, with no before and after,
But a lifetime burning in every moment
And not the lifetime of one man only
But of old stones that cannot be deciphered.

("East Coker")*

The first week of working on my papers has ended. I arrived here Wednesday before last, in the evening; Thursday and Friday to arrange my piled-
up material and correspondence; then work quite disoriented. The
feeling that I am re-entering a house abandoned in haste many years ago,
without anyone's having had a chance even to empty the ashtrays; the
stale atmosphere together with the heavy sensation of empty past time
seizes you by the nostrils; you feel flabby, with heavy, clumsy limbs.

Yesterday and today cloudy weather. The day before yesterday it
rained: a cloudburst. Winter draws nearer with infinite softness. The
"beauty" outside constantly interrupts you: a glance out the window;
the fragrance of autumn pine; the roaring of the wind. I'm afraid I must
start working, even during the day, with closed shutters and electric light:

Lands of the sun where you cannot see the sun,
lands of man where you cannot see man—

SUNDAY, OCTOBER 13

I woke up—for the first time in years—with a dream that filled me with
joy. I think that since the summer of '40 all my dreams have been public
nightmares.

In a foreign city, Paris or London. Evening. I stop and chat with a
tobacconist. The shop is lit with a white light. The feeling that with me
is a friend for whom I'm trying to find a room. The tobacconist is a

*T. S. Eliot, from "Four Quartets," in The Complete Poems and Plays, 1909-1950
(New York, Harcourt Brace Jovanovich, 1971; London, Faber and Faber), p. 129.

Greek "emigrant," a sympathetic and cheerful man. It is impossible for him to give me any useful information about the room I'm trying to find. "At least," I tell him, "isn't there someone who can rent me a room by the hour?" "If it's by the hour," he said, "I . . . " We part laughing. I continue along the wide sidewalk. I see (it is impossible to make out the face of the friend accompanying me) a car driven by American workmen or soldiers. We are impressed with the rapid motion of the front wheels, as if they were unfastened. "It must be the new Ford," I remark. In front of the car, which stops, is a bus—like those going to Kifissia, not the yellow ones. The bus doesn't move. The Americans get out; a brawl ensues; they're about to come to blows. People gather round. At the critical moment a streetcar also stops in front of the crowd. However, the street is not in Athens; it reminds me of the Boulevard Malesherbes in Paris. The streetcar conductor gets off holding a brass crank, very determined. He takes it upon himself to break them up. The Americans, the bus driver, and he advance, pushing the crowd aside, toward a gothic-style house. They enter, and suddenly I see them seated in tiers, each in a balcony, also gothic, attached to the facade of the house. From that position they discuss their case very calmly. The crowd below, myself among the crowd, look on. (I recall that I recently had gone out onto the balcony of our house, where I was seized with dizziness and shouted to Maró to hold me. I remember this and say: "Just look at them; I went out onto the balcony and got dizzy, and they talk up there totally unconcerned.") In a little while the difference is resolved, all come down, crowd and vehicles disperse, and I find myself on a bank of the Thames or in Venice, among actors dressed in motley costumes (green, red, and white) coming down toward the water, as if to embark, in unimaginably good spirits. An indescribable relief shudders through my heart. I wake up the moment that I say: "At last, I'm in Shakespeare's world!"

Never before, not for a good many years, have I waked up so light-hearted; my usual awakenings were those of a convict.

It's been drizzling all day long. The grace of this soft rain. The channel has taken on the softest nuances from gray to white—an old mirror. Clouds straddle the mountains surrounding. Through the window comes the live fragrance of pine.

Yesterday because of Eliot I was thinking of B. I met him on a Friday evening at the end of September. We dined together at Vasilainas' in Piraeus: Rex, Maurice Cardiff, Katsimbalis. B. is an incredible talking machine. One of the few Europeans left in Europe. A European by tradition too; he's a Hellenist. He speaks familiarly about poets, from Pasternak to Lorca, knows many apocryphal stories about famous men of his time. As Vasilainas serves without speaking, trying the customer's patience, B. charges on, spurring the company as in an attack. We discuss The Waste Land. A propos of "Mrs. Porter and her daughter," he says, "It was a whorehouse in Cairo; the one the Anzacs burned down (K. has told us this story many times). Mrs. Porter was the madam of this famous whorehouse, and the words of the song Eliot uses are not: "They wash their feet in soda water" but something much earthier.

MONDAY, OCTOBER 14

In the morning I rowed for an hour and a half, walked for two hours, and, on returning, the sun shining high, I swam. In the afternoon I slept. Myself has come out. It's very nice like this for the moment.

TUESDAY, OCTOBER 15

After breakfast, a twenty-minute walk on the hill behind the house. I read the pages of this notebook. Now it's ten o'clock. Truly the landscape absorbs you, just as Theophilos' landscapes absorb the figures (here see my notes on Theophilos).

And the wind that whispered with the lightning flashes of that
  autumn night
as the peaks of the Sleeping Maiden were wedged,
like the spike starting to turn red-hot, in the memory:
and if you condemn me to drink poison, I thank you;
your justice will be my justice, where can I go—

THURSDAY, OCTOBER 17

Yesterday, sunny until afternoon. I stayed at the shore all morning,

taking dips or reading the twenty-fourth book of the Iliad. When it grew
dark, a starry sky. At that moment John Craxton and L. Freud arrived,
two young artists I have been hearing about ever since I came here, and
whom I met only yesterday. They have been living on Poros for months
now; Lady Norton is their patroness. The former is an Englishman, the
latter, the grandson of the great Freud. They are enjoying Greece, where
they find things they don't have in their own countries: light, and a
different kind of human rapport, they say. They are also amused by
Karaghiozis, now playing in the village.* We all started out to go and see
it. The theater was closed; Alekos (the player's name) had gone to Athens
on "urgent business," as his assistant said; to console us he imitated with
guitar sounds a Stuka raid on a ship under way. On the way back
lightning and thunder began and a heavy downpour followed: very rich
flashes illuminating the sea. It rained all night long; in the morning Poros
was buried in a hyperborean fog; now at 9:00 the weather seems to be
improving. Fresh fragrances.

Deeply moved yesterday reading Achilles' speech to Priam. Astonishment:
this line is so firm and at the same time so sensitive, a vibrating chord.
Deeply moved also by the lofty art Homer has impregnated for others,
and which was there, as I read, a harmonious sound. Moreover, in Homer
everything meshes, the whole world is a woof of organic "umbilical cords";
the earthly, the heavenly world, animals, plants, elements, hearts of men,
good, evil, death, life—that ripen, vanish, and flower again. The mechanism
of the gods performs nothing supernatural, nothing ex machina; it
retains coherence, nothing else. I had observed something similar in '31
on Skiathos, when I reread the Odyssey from the beginning.

"Why do you wake the sleeping tear?" (Callimachus)†

"And naked to slaughter he is dragged by the feet." (18, 537, translated by
Solomos)‡

*The comic, hunchbacked, penniless, and cunning protagonist of the Greek shadow
theater.
†Callimachus, edited by Rudolph Pfeiffer (Oxford, 1949), Fragment 682, l. 447.
‡D. Solomos, Poiemata (Poems), ed. Linos Politis (Athens, 1948), l. 317.

FRIDAY, OCTOBER 18

Yesterday after lunch I cut wood. The body functions more easily; the
animal is more relaxed; no elation. That's it. The head is empty, emotions
settled down. Not at all in a poetic mood. It doesn't matter; for the
time being it's better so. Don't forget that you must leave and return.
Shut up rooms warp you with bad habits; the room where I lived in
recent years was stifling. I think of nothing now.

In the morning to the village with Mina. We climbed the narrow paths up
to the Clock. Friday is washday, clothes hanging out; you pass beneath
them to continue and feel them damp on your face. We returned by boat.
Rowing, cutting wood, swimming; clouds and sunshine. I don't want
to be anything today; tomorrow, we'll see.

Returning by boat we stopped near a sailboat, anchored in the open sea
far from the Galini. It came the day before yesterday to raise Aello, the
Benakis' sunken yacht. We said good morning and stayed there watching
preparations for the diver to submerge. We asked if Mr. Benakis was
coming. "It isn't Benakis' anymore," they told us. "He gave it to his maid,
and she has made an arrangement with our company. When we haul it
out she'll get about two hundred sovereigns." They were fastening the
markoutsi, as they called the air hose. On the gunwale, halfway down
from the bow, already wearing his suit, the diver sat on a small box. I had
imagined divers as being young, but this one must have been over sixty,
with a white mustache, his chin disappearing in the brass collar of his suit.
He said nothing but cast sidelong glances at the work of the others,
while carefully tying up the markoutsi himself. Enthroned, he was a
perfect example of a modern Poseidon. When the job was done, a sailor
brought him a cigarette, put it in his mouth, and lit it. All this without
a word. The others were testing the markoutsi; they finished as the
cigarette was finished. Then he got up and climbed down the small ladder;
they screwed on the helmet, and he disappeared into the blue water. We
followed his movements in the depths from the bubbles that surfaced.
He didn't stay down long; in a few minutes he was up, and they unscrewed
the helmet. He was not tired in the least; his face looked as if he were
returning from the café. Without raising his voice, he said sternly: "Fuck

your holy cross! Go bring the yacht and then send me down again."
The others, dumbstruck, said nothing.

SATURDAY, OCTOBER 19

Late last night Marouli, Lia, Lintsi, and Markos came in a small launch:
the Galini family. Athens atmosphere: the worries, the difficulty of finding
food, the longing to migrate. When this gets to you, you become suspended like a jellyfish drifting in the sea. Rotten foundations. Or worse.

MONDAY, OCTOBER 21

Marouli and company left today at dawn; Mina left too. About six, voices
woke me up: "The sun! The sun!"

I opened my eyes. By my bed was the pitcher from Aegina which I
brought to my room the other day (a big open poppy, surrounded by
green branches, painted on yellow clay); on the wall the sun's rays,
coming in parallel lines through the shutters, painted long, narrow, rose
streaks. I opened the window toward the sea beyond the Training Camp.
The huge disk of the sun, still bisected by the horizon, had a color I had
never seen before: it was the color of blackberry juice, a bit lighter. The
sea was breathless, without a ripple; the pine needles motionless as
sea-urchin spines in clear depths. On the horizon a black ship crawled very
slowly, just like on the Karaghiozis screen, underlined that amazing
disk, and vanished. Then, heels tapping on the wooden steps, suitcases,
words, fingers—they all left. (Writing this, I'm still drunk, with the un-
pleasant feeling of being a drunkard; only rarely and with difficulty can I
stand being drunk.)

I went out onto the veranda facing the sea; the time was now 8:30, the
sun high. It was impossible to separate the light from the silence, the
silence and light from the calm. Sometimes the ear would catch a noise,
a distant voice, a faint chirping. But these were in some way enclosed
elsewhere, like your heartbeat, felt for a moment and then forgotten. The
sea had no surface; only the hills opposite didn't end at the earth's rim,

but advanced beyond, below, starting all over again with a fainter image of their shape which vanished softly into faraway emptiness. There was a sense that another side of life exists. (I write with difficulty, trying to avoid generalizations, trying to describe the indescribable.) You perceived the surface of the water by watching the oars in the distance, as they dipped with a dry glitter like a windowpane struck by the sun; or again, later, when a boat passed below the house, its raised sails flapping, perfectly mirrored in the water like a picture on a deck of cards. The feeling that if the slightest crack opened up in this enclosed vision, all things could spill out beyond the four points of the horizon, leaving you naked and alone, begging alms, muttering imprecise words, without this amazing preciseness you had seen.

I returned to my room, dizzy, as I said, almost a visionary, and closed the east shutters, letting in only the dim light of the north.

Contours of mountains, contours of sounds.
Smoke under the nostrils of a god.
The leaf on a tree that is only a leaf is not a leaf.
And you are in a big house with many open windows,
and you run from room to room, knowing not from which to look out first
lest the pines leave . . .

In the night a dream: André Gide very old, in a cheap bar, in a camel's-hair overcoat, surrounded by two or three celestial youths of doubtful youth, terribly garrulous and gesticulatory. I was impressed by their odd-shaped skulls covered with disheveled hair colored almost dirty red or faded chestnut. Gide's lips were obviously rouged—I noticed this in particular. I don't know what we were talking about. I finished my sentence saying, " . . . Il est d'ailleurs très provincial." "Très certainement," he answered with weary calmness, "nous devenons tous des provinciaux." Later, as if there had been no interruption, I found myself at the National Theater. Maró went to get the tickets. We had no money and we asked for balcony seats. "Fifty and fifty are one hundred drachmas," I said. "We don't have one hundred drachmas to spend, and to think that last year I came here by car!" I was walking down the corridor with a heavy heart, when a checkroom woman who recognized me whispered "That's S." The whisper spread all around me from mouth to mouth. As I passed, people stepped aside and looked at me with respect, and I ascended, proudly now, to the balcony.

WEDNESDAY, OCTOBER 23

Yesterday and today, verse-making. Cavafy is waiting. The feeling that my fingers have hardened lamentably against writing verses; I've abandoned them for so many years. Military discharge, restoration: you thought it was the war, the difficult circumstances which would end with some sort of "peace." Suddenly you discover that you'll spend your entire life in disorder. It's all that you have; you must learn to live with it.

This light, this landscape, these days start to threaten me seriously. I close the shutters so I can work. I must protect myself from beauty, as the English from the rain and the Bedouins from the chamsin. You feel your brain emptying and lightening; the long day absorbs it. Today I understood why Homer was blind; if he had had eyes he wouldn't have written anything. He saw once, for a limited period of time, then saw no more. In Greece, alas, if you want to see all the time you must keep narrowing the diaphragm, as one does in photography. Otherwise you become a victim like the late Giannopoulos. (I have in mind of course the men who can see with their eyes.)

This morning at the lemon grove with Maró. At the beginning of the road a gravestone: "To Dr. Rothlauff of Bavaria, who fell, a victim to philanthropy, in 1837 on the plague-ridden Island of Calavria.* Erected by his colleagues."

In today's Vima I read a summary of Erasistratos' lecture. It ends with the sentence (in quotation marks in the newspaper): "(poetry or poets) offer the assurance that we who, like Vandals, besiege the self in us must know that this self of ours will not succumb." God help us!

*Calavria was the ancient name for Poros.

THURSDAY, OCTOBER 24 (7:15)

Son oeil ensorcelé découvre une Capoue
Partout où la chandelle illumine un taudis.

Poros is the Capua, the candle in my mind. I must escape from these
magic spells and apply myself to writing my lecture, otherwise I'll return
emptyhanded to the madness of Athens. There's still much work, work
to be done by the sweat of my brow. That's the trouble. I need time, and
I agonize over writing what little I write.

9:00. Somewhere a bell tolls. The sky cloudy today; the mood of Good
Friday. Death, pain, and misery must exist, unavoidably, on this day.
I said I'm in the mood to cry; I didn't lie.

The solution, if there is one, is never in the past, nor in stopping—keep
on going.

FRIDAY, OCTOBER 25

Yesterday was the first day I've felt tired. Since morning the southwest
wind. The wind's blowing carries me forcibly (yesterday and this morning)
to Skala: the Island of St. John, the cave and the fig tree (I see its shape
clearly), with votive rags tied to every twig. I am almost sickened with
sensibility.

Why does one write poems? Why, although they are such secret things
(for him who writes them), does he consider them more important than
anything else in life? This vital need.

Yesterday I made out of a walnut and a few acorns a small doll which I
named Mrs. Zen. It was impossible to do anything else.

Mrs. Zen

Contra tempo senza brio

Yesterday afternoon I stayed
alone in my room;

totally exhausted by
my wearying papers.
Washed out, I leaned
against my useless table
looking at a fly
play nervously

on the pane that cut me off
from the fresh air
and wrinkled the day.
In the light of dusk
the restless pines
recalled hands
seeking doves
that night when

unexpectedly,
in a horrid bed
lit by Hecate
I hugged dead Eros.
My fingers played
with a hollow walnut
and with an acorn
and another, smaller,

and some twigs I cut
along with a reed.
Like the cave of an octopus
slowly, slowly the mind
felt the tentacles unwind,
opening, spreading,
spreading, entwining
a body secretly;

the bent knees,
the sleeping fleece.

The wind grew stronger;
shallow my thoughts
descended, descended
toward the seashells,
the carved lips,
the closed-in music;

and these odds and ends
that I put together
with my fingers, kept
slipping away from me,
leaving nothing behind
but a little poison
and this tiny person
I call Mrs. Zen.

"You old fool, come out of it, get up and do something useful." (Kung).*

SATURDAY, OCTOBER 26

Yesterday morning verse-making; exercise on a given theme; very instructive. Contra tempo, observation of a line starting out from an insignificant beginning. Such exercises are necessary. Why does a pianist pound on his piano so many hours a day?

11:30. I've returned from the village after shopping. The feast of St. Demetrius. Schoolchildren outside in the Training Camp yard. The teacher—Charlie Chaplin type—giving orders. First the girls, then a flock of lambs with a black ram at its head (brilliant arrangement), then the boys. Gray sky, strong northeast wind. The "Pharasi"† that set sail at daybreak, we saw coming back. It had encountered a stormy sea outside, they told us.

*Ezra Pound, The Cantos (New York, 1973), XIII, 59.
†A nickname [meaning dustpan] we gave to an auxiliary ship of the Navy in the service of the Training Camp, because of the odd shape of its bow.—G. S.

Returning from town, a villager, his feet almost bare, said good morning. He started talking. The middle finger of his right hand "was eaten up," he says, "by arsenic, the poison that kills the locusts." He seems to be cold. "God is merciful," he says. His face looked crazy or drunk. The infinite fortitude of these people.

Yesterday, at sunset, a walk as far as the Diamantopoulos'. Autumn with all its charms. We went in to say good evening. We came out to winter. Incredible the rapid change of seasons in our country.

Zen problem: Take the "Sleeping Maiden" and put her in your bed, without ruffling either the bed or the mountainous curves of the "Sleeping Maiden."*

In a good mood since yesterday.

MONDAY, OCTOBER 28

At sea a ship's smoke on the horizon. The smoke rises straight up. The day holds its breath. Such calmness that every motion—a leaf, a sound, a boat in the canal—stays for a long time suspended in the light as if there were no end. In the morning I cut wood, then swam; it's now 11:00. I'm writing in my room, which I filled with shadows when I was battering like a bat entangled in desires and plans, as difficult as a Zen problem. It's strange (for me) to have any feeling for this sack full of "personal sentiments" that is now loosened and drives me mad (literally) with these unsettled winds. I had kept them all tightly shut up during the war years, for six years at least. Now they burst forth with the force of a violent spring in northern climes. Where will they possibly join the other self? The one, let me simply say, who expresses himself.

The character of houses. Houses, too, have lineage. This morning I thought I missed Marouli around here; but the house makes her presence felt, with her whims and her unrestrained reactions. The rooms, the

*The Sleeping Maiden (Koimomeni) is the popular name of the mountain Ortho-lithion on the Argolic peninsula. Seen from Poros, its outline resembles a woman sleeping.

corridors, the stairs, the drawers, some trivia—demand her presence like a kitten that has lost its master.

Maybe it's Poros, too. Here everything seems stationary, haunted somehow. I suspect one cannot last long in this state. It is Calypso's island; you must decide to abandon it some day for rocky Ithaca. Hardly had I written these words, when an army of rebelling sentiments started roaring within me: Hannibal at Capua.

THURSDAY, OCTOBER 31

Yesterday to the Poseidon,* then to Vagionia. The sea to the north motionless as in summer. Swimming. The shore was covered with foam and flotsam (I have never before seen so much): roots of reeds, strangely polished driftwood, corks, a paradise of playthings for me. I put in my knapsack many of these silent objects. We left at 10:00 and returned at 16:00; a good walk.

The poem I've been writing since a week ago last Tuesday, with sudden flaring up and dying down, like green wood burning in our fireplace, tires me at times. This morning I've been wandering around since 7:00 disorganized, fumbling with my hands, creating objects and trying to give them familiar forms, carving a cypress wand I cut yesterday. The smell of this wood, its architecture and color, fill me with delight. A feeling of the waste of the life I lead in Athens has been very intense since yesterday. Any field whatsoever around here would make me a thousand times more human than the Athenian jungle. Intense need (yesterday and today) to give up the Ministry and all that prattling; no longer just to gain time to write literature, but to mature and die like a man.

Evening. In the afternoon I cut wood until it grew dark. I returned home sweating, my hands coated with resin. A bath, and then I sat at my table. I finished the poem. Title: "Thrush." I don't know if it's good; I know that it's finished. Now it must dry.

*The temple of Poseidon on Poros where the Athenian orator Demosthenes pursued by the Macedonians took poison and died in 322 B.C.

FRIDAY, NOVEMBER 1

Copying "Thrush," and making minor corrections. From 10:00 on,
half-naked, I cut wood. It's November, yet I dipped in the sea three times.
I think the ending of the poem isn't bad (Part III) because it's well
sustained by the first two parts and at times it comes close to the preciseness I want. As for the last lines of that part, the allegro, I would call
it, or the "lyric," others would (a tone that I haven't used for several
years), this is strange: before I left yesterday afternoon for the garden,
I left on my table very obscure verses (emotionally, I mean); the tone was
constantly diminishing. Coming down from the mountain I thought
of Bashō's teaching to Kikakou:*

"We shouldn't abuse God's creatures. You must reverse the haiku,
not:
A dragonfly;
remove its wings—
pepper tree.
but:
A pepper tree;
add wings to it—
dragonfly."

When I picked up the pen again, I did reverse the lines I had written; this
was the right tone.

Yesterday:

      Dr. Rothlauff and Mrs. Zen

Dr. Rothlauff smokes his cigarette, looking at the strait of Poros.
Mrs. Zen is provocative, creation of a pauper's imagination.
Dr. Rothlauff shoves his hat back and rests his cane on an oyster.
Mrs. Zen seeks to tear the world to shreds; her head is a pierced walnut.
Dr. Rothlauff with myopic eyes discerns in the sea dregs strange, and
    sometimes important, things.

*Les Haikai de Kikakou, textes et commentaires japonais traduits pour la première
fois par Kuni Matsuo et Steinilber-Oberlin (Paris, 1927), p. xi.

Mrs. Zen holds sword and shield; she wears a tassled helmet.

Dr. Rothlauff is immaculate; his overcoat is camel's hair, cigarette
Papastratos No. 2.

Mrs. Zen (the fortune-teller said) will have an eye for the handsome lad
who'll warm her in the cold.

Dr. Rothlauff continues unsuspecting, stupid, fascinated with fish that
dance and leap—

Pluck the petals of a daisy, Mathios: they'll meet? . . . they won't meet?
. . . they'll meet? . . .

SATURDAY, NOVEMBER 2

One cannot easily tear oneself away from a poem which is finished; the
fibers can't be cut easily. All day long I've still been fumbling with the
"Thrush": finishing touches, corrections, additions of fine tones. I still
feel bruised by the poem. It has drawn heavily on my experience of life in
the past years and on ideas for verses jotted down at random since last
January.

This morning: wood, swimming. A fisherman passed and offered fish; his
boat is a kourita. Here people do not know these boats. Those I asked
said "something like a gondola." I, too, asked him: "What do you call
your caique?" "Kourita," he answered. I understood that he was from
Asia Minor. I asked him other questions, knowing what he would answer,
and was pleased that he said what I expected. "Does she go by sail?"
"Yes, she soars; I came from Smyrna on her, from the Englezonesi . . . "
"Without a keel, do you use leeboards?" "These don't need leeboards;
with the sail, their side serves as a keel . . . from Smyrna to here? . . .
This one went to Egypt in 1913 with four or five others; she's the only
one that came back. They took them to the Nile and sold them. Look
at her warped planks." I looked. I was pleased with the workmanship, the
beautiful old wood. The carvings on prow and stern recalled icons from
my past. I observed this boat with much joy.

SUNDAY MORNING, NOVEMBER 3

I've been here almost a month. Essentially, by nature I must be a man like Rodakis (of the house on Aegina), caring or molding his house all his life. The poems would be extra—gifts of God.

There's been no electricity since the day before yesterday; the fuses are burnt out. Today we tell Evangelia about the mishap. She replies: "In my sleep I saw you distressed; this must be it." It's natural that the language of dreams pertains even to trifles; messengers condescending even to humble errands. The intellectuals have made them speak only with the trumpet of Jericho or with bagpipes.

   Ariadne

Your lips were beautiful, and you liked the olive
you bit; the red, the russet, and the black
blend well when the hand stretches out to the noose
and frees the dog, the hare, and the bull.

And the animals gleam warm in the enclosed day.
And, all together, knotted braids, clasped limbs,
teeth in the blackberries and thorny shrubs,
and fingers caressing the light like an eel

of gold piercing the sky's white dome—
And all together sway at the edge of the abyss,
without coherence, without ego, and the mountain peaks
that woke up so jagged, and your brackish body

dancing, dying, dancing again,
and the reeds nailed to the angry delta
Stut-ter-ring th-read hea-vy to-orch la-lab-la-
byrinth; alpha, beta, gamma, delta . . .

MONDAY, NOVEMBER 4

Yesterday noon Akron came (he left this morning), and with him the rabid atmosphere of Athens. All day today I chopped wood: like Rodakis.

TUESDAY, NOVEMBER 5

The cyclamen become deeper and deeper in color as winter approaches. With more character.

In essence, the poet has one theme: his live body.

WEDNESDAY, NOVEMBER 6

I am still writing the essay on Cavafy which I started on Monday; I mean the final version. At one o'clock I gave it all up and jumped into the sea. The atmosphere does not aid critical thought; everything dances.

FRIDAY, NOVEMBER 8

Yesterday, like Rodakis, I made a mermaid out of cedar; great joy. Before I lay down I sat and looked at her for a long time.

I am constantly trying to finish this unfortunate lecture, but criticism, any criticism, becomes totally insubstantial here.

Afternoon, 17:00. A strong southwest wind is blowing and it's raining. Suddenly a rainbow in the east, exactly perpendicular to the point where the sun rises. In the west a huge curtain of yellow flame turns to iodine behind the violet mountains. In between, the sea with gray and green tones and the houses with the patina of a great craftsman.

SATURDAY, NOVEMBER 9

An amazing day: not a cloud, not even a breath. The smoke of Abel rises straight up, vertically. The sea, wherever a man touches it, breaks and glitters like glass. At night a full moon; the same calmness; only the light is green or dark blue—the tone of dawn. The huge mass of the mountain opposite, all its folds apparent, is mirrored in the lagoon vanishing in the shadow. The lights of Poros are like candles. There's a feeling of enclosed space, of an empty church with the cold marble shadows in the dome evoking profound awe. This can happen anywhere outside the earth, within the universe.

SUNDAY, NOVEMBER 10. 6:30

The crack of dawn. Yesterday's moon is still very bright high in the west.

The motionless agility of these things is such that you think the ship in which we are sailing can capsize at any moment, dumping you into the whirlpool, together with stones, wood, colors, boats—like a huge ocean liner sinking.

You need to narrow the diaphragm more and more; otherwise you're lost.

THURSDAY, NOVEMBER 14

Yesterday after lunch a sneak attack on the steps of the Galini by an M.L. of the Royal Navy, and unexpectedly John Lehmann, Rex, Cardiff, and George K. appeared. L. asked to visit me at Poros, and the government—which treats him superbly—offered him—what irony—a warship! Now the local authorities have changed their attitude toward me; they accept me. This morning all together to Hydra, to Nikolis' house, then swimming with R. Perfect weather and ease on this little ship. On Hydra the feast of St. Constantine the Hydriot, who suffered martyrdom on Rhodes. I feel great sympathy for this household island saint.

As the days go by I feel cleaner.

MONDAY, NOVEMBER 18

I continue the essay on Cavafy, which I find difficult at times. Some nights I have the impression that I am wasting my time. However, at last I have found a rhythm here: the night's tired thought in the morning becomes an idea for expanding a little further.

TUESDAY, NOVEMBER 19

Terribly exhausted last night. I read my essay to Maró. Finished, it seemed tasteless. Today I worked on it again all day, paying attention to its articulations. In the evening I read it to Maró again. So this too is finished.

TUESDAY, NOVEMBER 26. DAWN

The light, deep cherry red, like a curtain falling through a long crack between the clouds. The one I mark horizontally (in red) in the sketch.

MONDAY, DECEMBER 2

Dr. Rothlauff, Mrs. Zen, Andromeda, the King of Asine, yesterday became a heap on the piece of furniture I was using for a book case; the images of mashed up mankind we are trying to rediscover; tomorrow we leave for Athens. The day before yesterday I finished copying my lecture on Cavafy. It was high time. If I had another forty days of quiet, the book, too, would be finished, I think. I would rid myself of that burden as well. Now I'm leaving Poros with this essay and the "Thrush," which are still drying. I put a lot into them, but don't know what their worth is.

I leave Poros as I left Crete in May 1941—for the unknown. The great calmness I have felt here lately, in the mornings, I don't know whether I'll find it again. It seemed like a kind of transgression.

I also leave with certain "ideas" about the light. It is the most important thing I've "discovered" since the ship that brought me home entered Greek waters (Hydra, October 1944). "The King of Asine" expresses some of this, the "Thrush" something of it also. But I don't know if I'll ever be able to express this essential as I feel it, this foundation of life. I know I must live with the light. I know nothing further; I don't know whether I'll succeed. The only thing I understood here is that no problem can be solved by marking time; you must forge ahead or break.

The day before yesterday under my northern window I saw two shy little blossoms on an almond tree—the first almond tree in blossom. On the mountain the cyclamen turn to leaves; in the sea, the dark blue fluttering of the kingfisher.

I give thanks.

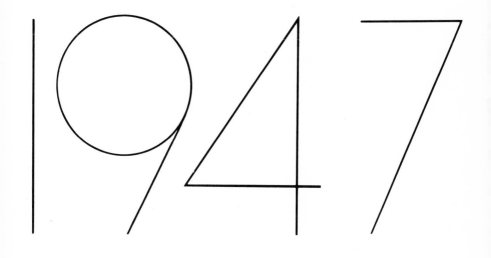

NIGHT OF DECEMBER 31–JANUARY 1. ATHENS

Here, since Tuesday, December 3. On the streets the sounds of pipes and whining songs: carols. There's an intense feeling of the psychic disintegration of men. They talk to you and you feel you're reaching into a ragged fog. Terrible lack of cohesion, of coherence, of consequence: nowhere can you have any confidence: horror.

Now the Ministry doesn't know what to do with me. Each time I ask to see the personnel director (since the 5th of last month) they tell me he is sick. I work hard, sometimes wearily, on the Cavafy book; a stagnating sensibility blunts my efforts. When talking with M. about our lack of money (justified, actually), I calculate that, apart from my job, I work ten hours a day without earning anything. Literature is for free in Greece; that's why it's ridiculed. I have courage.

The other night at Psaras' to bid farewell to Captain Michalis who left yesterday. I drank a lot; I needed it. On the way back he was holding Joan with one hand and, with the other, an enormous gourd of superb patina, sent to him from Crete, which he takes everywhere filled with retsina. He was singing "Filentem."

On Tuesday, December 17, I gave my lecture on Cavafy and Eliot at the Institute. Many people, including even Sikelianos. One and a half women fainted. Few understood; more were enthusiastic. The foreigners were impressed by the presence of so many young people. The usual mishmash in the newspapers: A "Sidonian youth" thought to give the following headline to his petty quibble: "Tuesday, an inauspicious day."

A few days ago I borrowed Gide's Theseus. This so-alive old man is one of the very few bright promontories left in Europe. Reading about the meeting of Theseus with Oedipus, I thought of the ending of the "Thrush": "obscurité tu seras ma lumière."

I am terribly amused by Gregory of Nazianzus whom I'm reading now; I took the volumes of Migne from Grandpa's library.* What brio; I try to imagine these three—Gregory, Basil, Julian—as students in Athens. Dreadful idiosyncracies, incompatible, and yet all in the same boat of those times.

SATURDAY, JANUARY 18

A sunset made up of a very few hues in the clouds and the snow-covered mountains, accented with green.

Tragic beauty: only now do I begin to understand this ineffable thing— words barely scratch its surface.

MONDAY, JANUARY 20

For almost a month now I have been working poorly; for many reasons,

*Jacques Paul Migne (1800–1875), French priest and publisher of Greek and Latin religious texts.

including Athens. The fever of the sick city and at the same time the feeling of a beauty or a vivacity or an acceptance; a pillar of light before me refuses to let me articulate a word. It's a pity I had no time left on Poros to finish this study (of Cavafy). And I don't know what's in store for me.

At noon Rex called to say that he has finished the translation of the "Thrush." He went to work with great enthusiasm. We began last Wednesday at his house, in Psychiko. I gave him an extemporaneous oral translation. By Saturday he had already written the first part. "It's strange," he told me, "yesterday as I was writing, the janitor came in—he goes hunting occasionally— and brought me a thrush. A good omen. I wanted to call you." He's the first translator who hasn't tormented me. Ancient Greek, which he knows, helps him of course, and perhaps even more so, the mastery of his own language.

TUESDAY, JANUARY 21

Nothing moves, nothing moves.

A lecture on "Samson Agonistes" at the British Institute. It was raining on the way—wet trees; a square window with glowing faces.

Two in the morning. Touti rages; she's frantic (in heat). Her black fur takes on the glitter of an electric spark; when you touch her she's like a knot of shivers; poor humans.

WEDNESDAY, JANUARY 22

Touti, the black mirror, reflects my dispositions, as after our return from Poros, the melancholy feeling of being a prisoner. I wonder at times when she will fall into the black pit she herself makes in the light of day.

These days she is seized by the erotic orgasm of January. For two nights she wouldn't let us sleep. She kept twisting, rolling, kneading her claws, howling—that brisk meowing. Yesterday we brought her a tomcat. He hid in a corner and remained motionless from the afternoon until noon today. Touti's flirting and frenzies didn't move him. We took her into the garden. A gray tomcat came along, an alley-cat from the nearby taverna. He watched her and she rolled in front of him in the sleet, in the mud, as if it were burning grass. Her beautiful fur had turned into a wretched, muddy rag. And yet he was her destiny.

SATURDAY, JANUARY 25

Yesterday at noon I lunched with Rex at Psychiko. Early in the afternoon, a walk beyond the Tourkovounia, as far as the Omorphi Ekklesia. He told me about his early endeavors, the difficulty of publishing his first book. Then, "I don't much care about reviews now, except for the Times Literary Supplement; they're all favorable." We talked about the manner of composition. I said, "I know how I can finish something if I have its final sentence in my mind." "The beginning and the end are the most difficult," he said. There is something solid about this man; I feel a steadily growing friendship for him.

My weakness (and occasionally strength) of never being able to concentrate on one thing alone. This, too, as I go along, grows steadily.

WEDNESDAY, JANUARY 29

In the evening a dinner for Sir Ronald Adam, a general, now head of the British Council. The General talks endlessly about UNESCO. The repetition of this Romanian-sounding word revolves in our conversation like a bothersome fly. "They've decided," he says, "to draw up lists of translators. So authors can be sure that their works will be translated by the best translators." Splendid!

SUNDAY, FEBRUARY 2

Yesterday and today galley proofs of the "Thrush." I've lost much time since the end of December. Tarousopoulos, the printer (not Petros, the other one), whom I begged to speed up the job so that we could finish, said to me: "What thrushes and blackbirds are you talking about? I'm busy printing the minutes of the Academy now."

THURSDAY, FEBRUARY 6

Ghikas at the house; he's making a sketch of me for Lehmann's edition of my poems.*

SATURDAY, FEBRUARY 8

Since yesterday morning with too many bishops at Grandpa's, etc. Even now cassocks flutter in my mind. I'm no longer surprised that everything we do becomes faded.

SUNDAY, FEBRUARY 9

To Marousi and from there to Kifissia at Mrs. K.'s. Old Maria is very sick; they talk about her as if she were going to pass away in a few hours. The house is sad, cut off from the outside world; the telephone doesn't work; it was cold. I was almost glad that we had to wait in a long line for the return bus, to be in contact with people who stood on their feet and talked.

The Palamas Prize†: any affair, even the slightest, now becomes an open sewer—even this one. The stench grabs you by the throat.

Death is wise; just think, if it didn't exist, so many wretched things would be perpetuated. This purgation is a relief. Surely, other wretched things will harass those who live after us, but their blood also will be newer and perhaps, one thinks, will allow them to overcome the wretchedness.

TUESDAY, FEBRUARY 11

At Mrs. K.'s. Old Maria is even worse, if possible. An ambulance was waiting at the garden; they're moving her to Evangelismos Hospital. Old

*George Seferis, The King of Asine and Other Poems, translated from the Greek by Bernard Spencer, Nanos Valaoritis, Laurence Durrell, with an introduction by Rex Warner (London, 1948).
†The Palamas Prize was established in 1943 in honor of the poet Kostis Palamas (1853–1943). Seferis was awarded the prize on February 26, 1947.

Sophia, Cappadocia stock that ripens and endures like a tree. Then the doctor came, a young man talking in a loud voice. All the others were so weak that his voice seemed like a small typhoon in the cold and melancholy house. Then the stretcher; they lifted the fleshless old woman like a plane-tree leaf. The white car with red crosses, a wound amidst the pines, something very harsh against the background of Hymettus.

WEDNESDAY

And yet in the background is this pillar of light, this untouched thing that remains wedged in the heart of change like a diamond in a brook. There is a dreadful affirmation of one's whole being in such moments, like a Bach chorale, you think, that continues, irrevocably; you know that even if they suddenly machine-gunned instruments·and musicians and listeners it would not stop. I feel now that this exists behind the best of what I've written (whether or not apparent). Around this pivot, this thread, my functioning images and their shadows are crystallized. Hard to say this with precision; I should write a poem. It is similar to the expression—it's just occurred to me—perfectly applicable to a kind of sudden and indestructible humaneness. Prometheus' cry "O sacred ether"* had a similar effect on me when I read it one chilly afternoon in Johannesburg and burst into an exile's sobs. The same with Makriyannis' words: "And you don't hear us, and you don't see us"—or his talk at Mega Spelio. The same with certain moments of the war, in the face of danger.

Adverse moments are not moments of discouragement; even when this feeling is not at its height, I know the untouchable thing exists. There may be moments of endurance, sometimes of agonizing search, sometimes of sarcastic defense of the organism in the face of disgust. This is not the dead end; the dead end, still worse, is the consciousness of a standstill.

THURSDAY

Something like an Argonaut expedition with many Clashing Rocks—those

*Aeschylus, Prometheus Bound, l. 88.

stones that strike you, now on the head, now in the heart, now in the kidneys. Ultimately they never finish you off. You rise half-dead and keep going, a foolish visionary in the golden light of the sea.

The golden fleece. I imagine that the Argonauts, as they went along, now and then uttered foolish cries. Like the rhythm of the chorale, which is such a voyage.

Foolish cries, but definite. I remember those days on Poros and my impatience when I heard: "How beautiful! What a marvel! What magic!" In the evening I read the newspaper as if I were uncovering a miserable wound. This light and this wound; this coming and going between the light of day and man's tragedy that twists your entrails: the marriage of heaven and hell, that's the passion of a beautiful day. You must be very alive and have crushed your ribs on many Clashing Rocks to retain this passion. You must have loved life like a man who has retained within him, throughout all his ages, the child he once was.

Not like a one-man-band. What an impression he made on me; I saw him a few times in the very old days. The big drum on his back, the bagpipe bellows under his arm, the bells on his hat and ankles. Above all the spasmodic inhuman movements. How many are like him? You forget them; when you find them again, you recognize at once the worn-out tune and spasmodic movements of an insect caught in a spider's web. You seek the live bodies and the chorale, the horror and the sublimity, the irrevocable force of germination that breaks rocks. My God, what happens to all these inside the one-man-band, behind the bells that wound us like thorns!

We've cast grace out of our life; that's what we lack. That which I saw once before in Spatharis, the Karaghiozis-player. He came to my home hungry, in despair. Yet how he talked! "The roof is leaking, Sir. We have no electricity. People get married in airplanes, but we have no electricity. Now the chimney lamp breaks, now the kerosene is diluted. And my home, you see, is a workshop. As it grows dark, black thoughts seize me. Then I grab paper and chisels, and I make Kopritis, Bitsikokos, Karaghiozis."

Something I myself can't do. When I hear such men, I'm ashamed that I do so little.

SATURDAY, FEBRUARY 22

Vacation is not trouble-free. The feeling that everything wounds and creates a sick, wretched condition; you feel that you are losing blood, that you are at the mercy of the first strong wave. Dreadful, how little our land nourishes us—no, it's not the land's fault.

WEDNESDAY, FEBRUARY 26

They gave me the Palamas Prize for poetry. They talked for days about the terrible political scandal that would occur if I accepted it. Miserable creatures, self-appointed journalists, who try with mud and bile to atone for their wretchedness in the times of the Germans, and swell the heads of various fools or scoundrels. (Haima and Hestia came out saying the Prize is German. Who says this? The man at Energitiki.) This whole affair so filled me with disgust that I got carried away by the activities of some of my friends, it's outrageous. (Under any stone you lift in Greece today, you'll find abomination; lucky for you it isn't horror. It's an effort to maintain my equilibrium.)

FRIDAY, FEBRUARY 28

First day of spring, a morning of Hymns of Praise among the garden trees. This sensation I have of feeling myself a "poet" is new. I mean, poet in the raw, of such sensitivity, such pulsing in the midst of life. I don't at all know whether this means that I'll be able to write better poems.

MARCH 15

They'll take from you the shadow of the trees, they'll take it,
They'll take from you the shadow of the sea, they'll take it,
They'll take from you the shadow of the heart, they'll take it,
They'll take your shadow . . .

SATURDAY, MARCH

Epilogue: A prize in today's Athens = a Niagara of muck.

APRIL 6, PALM SUNDAY

In March I worked steadily and hard every day (the Ministry uses me now for subordinate jobs which I do at home), I can't complain; it's better.

I've finished the poems "of setting out for Ithaca." Now it's more difficult. The feeling you have after the effort of the pen finding the groove in the paper is gone. The situation around me is unhealthy—damned, I should say —in this morass of souls and bodies to which Greece has been reduced. You think indeed that at times everything is spinning incoherently. They insult, yell, are scurrilous with constantly accelerating frenzy, and yet there's no end to it. The distance from here to the point where you yourself won't be able to keep your sanity is minimal. A strange psychology is created within you, to hold on to whatever is alive—a body, a kitten, a tender shoot, anything, in short, that has a throb of truth. You feel an unrestrained desire to howl to God, or to something that must exist above this thick mire: "Don't you hear us? Don't you see us?" And then you wonder: must I perhaps be punished because I insist on not becoming like the others; for this hubris.

Last night I stayed out late with friends. At Psaras' and then to a patisserie at Omonia until two in the morning. I think it must be the first time I have stayed out at night like this since last January. I listened to their discussions—art, politics, social events—trying to put together what they wanted to say. Impossible; words kept leaping into my ears—outbursts of profundity, anger, or cleverness, without coherence, that stopped unexpectedly with an exclamation or somebody's joke. Then silence, and the thing began all over again.

I could face all this, the hell with it, if I had the means (that is, only the daily bread for my wife and me) to devote myself to the work I want and know I can do—so that I wouldn't be working like a crippled man. The degradation of money. Yesterday I had the most humiliating idea I may ever have had in my life: to stop writing for a period of time—five or ten years, I don't know—to find a job that would allow me to save a little money, and then do what I want: a ridiculous thought; for living things there's no deferment.

In the morning we went to Ghikas' and watched King George's funeral. From the window we could see a fairly large part of Metropolis Square. In the narrow street below the cannon carriage was waiting empty, with sailors getting ready to pull it. The solemn movement, the stylized ceremony. At a moment, when the crown glittered in the sun's light, the feeling that all coincidences, adventures, virtues, vices, heroisms, grandeurs, hatreds, bile, and so much blood, and so much longing were lined up to form a pyramid beneath this small, so impersonal point, were leading into an irrevocable order, with no cause or effect, revealing the tragic condition of man, who has no other capacity, one might say, than the capacity for inexhaustible suffering. A nightmare until the moment when the tail end of the procession had vanished, and the regular passersby started coming and going again, bringing back once more the everyday anarchy of life.

APRIL 12, HOLY SATURDAY

Such a winter has begun that yesterday people said "Merry Christmas" at the Epitaphios.* In the morning to Piraeus; we were waiting for Nanis' arrival on the <u>Corinthia</u>. On the same boat Henri Michaux, too, returning from Egypt. We left N. at the Grande Bretagne. Its luxury in this desolate place stands out as truly Ptolemaic. After lunch I met Michaux at Akron's; he was going to re-embark in a little while. Short, slim, featherlike, with thinning, straight blond hair; on his mouth sarcasm, sensuality, bitterness. His wife a down-to-earth person, a bit like a

*The evening service on Good Friday in commemoration of Christ's entombment; the gold-embroidered or painted pall with its representation of Christ's burial is placed beneath the sepulcher canopy for veneration; the entire edifice, adorned with flowers, is carried outside the church in a procession.

steamroller beside him. He was autographing his books when I came in. Awkward, hasty talk; they all were looking at their watches. He had disembarked in order to see the Acropolis.

He said "Acropolis" as someone would say the name of a heraldic animal. I told him that ten years ago I had translated a piece of his: "Which one?" " 'Je vous écris d'un pays lointain.' " "It's my best," he said, "I don't know if I'll be able to write another like it."

The trouble with such brief meetings is that you don't know exactly what the words mean.

Then, I think because of Gide's lecture on him, he asked: "Can you give lectures? . . . I . . . look . . . it depends . . . I should be able to enter a hall, look at the audience, pick out someone, and say: 'Toi, mon vieux . . . I must put certain things in your head.' And start talking." "What if you don't happen to find anyone?" I asked. "Eh! Then I should be able to leave without saying anything."

He also said: "A writer, if he has one reader, is not a writer; if he has two readers, he's not a writer; but if he has three readers (stressing the word three as if it were many thousands), eh! then we can say he's a writer."

Later: "The only thing we can do, that we have a duty to do, is to express evil (le mal), here, like this!" And he pointed at his little book on the table, Liberté d'action, which I haven't read.

TUESDAY, MAY 6

A dream: confused recollection: At Nikis Street an eviction of Jews. Their things on the sidewalk, somewhere near the Pyramides pastry shop, and a curtain representing Moses. Then a reception somewhere, a movie in this reception showing Bikini or Polynesia. Then on the deck of a small ship, sailing through a very narrow canal, with house fronts right and left. As we were going along, a naked woman in a window and someone who remarked indifferently: "En bateau, on s'introduit mieux dans l'intimité des gens."

FRIDAY

Returning home late last night, through the Zappeion, I heard, from the direction of the corner of the Radio Station, a woman screaming: "You've killed me, you've finished me, stop it now." I ran, trying to see from afar. A body was rolling on the ground, and a man was bent over it, beating it. Three or four policemen and two or three passersby looked on indifferently.

The woman shouted, writhing on the ground: "Why do you whip me when I had my card inspected this morning?" I was beside myself. "Why are you beating her?" I asked a lieutenant angrily. "We're not beating her," he replied; "I was right behind you and I didn't see anyone beating her." "Can't four men handle a woman," I said, "must they beat her?" I was impressed with the apathy of the spectators. They were ordinary people. "Don't get angry, Mister," someone said, "she's a whore." The woman was obviously now going through a fit of hysterics. As they were taking her to the police station, without beating her anymore, she would sit down on the ground every five steps, scream and lift up her clothes, revealing her nakedness, to show the bruises. "I'm a prostitute, is that why they have to whip me? It's the pimp's fault—I'll show him!" I was impressed by both the cruelty and the cowardice of the men beating her. When I started shouting they put their tails between their legs. Strange my psychological participation in this scene.

MAY 22, POROS

The Aello: her hull alone at last, since this past fall. The figurehead on the prow: a worm-eaten eagle (the worms of the depths) with red sores. Only one wing; the other eaten away.

En route to Troezen. The dried-up torrent, with arid boulders, white like skulls on scarecrows; smell of elecampane.

MAY 23, POROS

At Tompazis' house:

"The frames of these eight paintings of the Battle of Navarino were made from the wood of the first three dead tangerine trees in Greece, which had been given in the year 1829 by Admiral Heyden, the Russian Commander at Navarino, to Manolis Tompazis, having been detached together with their pots from the flagship Azof, where they were during the sea battle of Navarino on February 8/20 1827."*

MAY 30, ATHENS

Our public life is a jungle where everyone is out to slaughter the other with guile, slander, cowardice, shamelessness. These people make you feel as though you were chewing fog.

FRIDAY, JUNE 20

Since the middle of May I've been swimming in public sewers.

Nanis left Monday at nine. He was drowned by everything as soon as he arrived in Greece. He became like a cork bobbing in the harbor amid uprooted seaweed and melon rinds. This thoughtful man could find nothing within himself to hold onto in the whirlwind of Greece. He wilted like a flower taken out of a greenhouse into the frost. He left with permanent panic in his soul. My poor friend.

SUNDAY, JUNE 22

Since morning at Kifissia, at Polemon's. We returned and ate here. I drag myself around. The violin from the nearby taverna torments me with gypsy tunes. I translated a few pages from Rex's lecture (anonymously, for the money).

WEDNESDAY, JULY 2

In bed since the evening of Tuesday the 24th: kidneys. The doctors

*The Battle in the Bay of Navarino was fought on October 20, 1827, when the Turkish and Egyptian fleets were annihilated by the joined naval squadrons of Russia, France, and England. This decisive battle established the independence of Greece.

order complete rest. For a week now I have been hearing the little bell which warns that the clepsydra is emptying.*

SUNDAY, JULY 6

Letter from Romilly Jenkins about the "Thrush." He wonders if, when I wrote the line: "And if you sentence me to drink poison, I thank you," I had in mind the "terrific line" of Lear: "If you have poison for me, I will drink it."

It must be ten years since I've read King Lear, and no matter how hard I search nowhere can I find any trace of this line. The line in "Thrush" is an intentional reference to the Apology of Socrates, and the association with the English I now believe to be an error; it doesn't fit my meaning at all; but, the competent reader has his rights.

TUESDAY, JULY 8

Today to Pammakaristos Clinic for X-rays. The first time I've gone out since I fell sick. The plate shows a stone in the right kidney. This reminds me of something we so often forget: that we exist because every so often someone decides to grant us a deferment of punishment. But had I forgotten it so completely? When I recall last fall on Poros the indescribable thrill that overwhelmed me every moment, that unconquerable intoxication with every living thing.

THURSDAY, JULY 10

This one, the man who is controlled by his will, who is patient, and prudent, and acts with the wisdom at his disposal. And this other, the man who is mad about whatever suits him, for an affirmation of life, who is ready to risk everything he has, driven by a "logic" of another kind, which is omnipotent, which tells him that otherwise nothing can be held firm, that everything will vanish like a handful of dry sand through

*The device used by the ancient Greeks to measure time by marking the regulated flow of water through a small opening.

his fingers—the cohabitation of these two, not at all a cohabitation of angel and beast (in each there exists both the angelic and the bestial), sometimes bearable, sometimes a tragedy. And the third man who watches, prays, hoping that neither of them will be destroyed.

A strange phenomenon of my illness (coincidental or otherwise, I don't know) is a sudden and amazing sensitivity of smell. On Tuesday, the night I had the attack, an ordinary smell assumed an oppressive magnitude. The other night, seated in the bedroom, as the wind shifted southerly, I heard the smell of the sea through the window. Maró, who has a better sense of smell than I, smelled nothing.

Just now a card from Nanis in Italy. A photograph of the Villa d'Este, it says: "Questa è una feeria delle chimere." Classification of men according to the chimera each pursues; these chimeras hiding under the calmest surface would create another breed of fauna. Nanis' chimera is the world of conveniences, of retreats of little or much luxury, of orderly and banklike stability. How can he live in Aeolia? Without a minimum of such conditions, he sickens and loses his bearings, just as the dress of a proper lady becomes sleazy and wrinkled at critical moments, her make-up abominable. And he has so many virtues, this rare man.

FRIDAY, JULY 11

It seems more difficult to get to see a doctor than a prime minister. After three days of waiting, at last, tomorrow. An additional burden; and this, on a ship already loaded to the scuppers.

I think that lately—a long time has passed—I have suffered the worst that could have happened to me in the times we live in: a flood of sensitivity makes me feel as if, stripped of protective skin, I'm wandering about with open wounds. Dust, flies, awkward gestures—all very painful. From deep down, I long for the days I could sometimes control this sensitivity with grace. It was not of lesser quality. Was I stronger? Yet I feel this condition is not sickness; it's an ardent affirmation of life. There's no lack

of courage, the calm surface hasn't changed, but a terrible effort is
needed, which makes me lamentably heavyhearted.

The third tirade (this year) in a row since the beginning of the month has
burst out against me. The first pretext, the Palamas Prize; the second,
the Theophilos exhibit. And now, "The Clique." My God! It's no longer
the art-lovers-who-traveled-and-saw-the-museums of the venomous afternoon newspaper, but Mr. —. He insults and spits like a hysterical lackey
and at the same time invokes Epictetus to declare that he's stoically sober
while the others are drunk. And just think, his grand title is the "critical
spirit." Where is the spirit? Where is the critic? Guarda e passa.

SATURDAY, JULY 12

I go to bed very late these days—it's the only way to sleep till morning.
Heavy heat. Between midnight and two are the best moments of the day.
But when you open your eyes the dreams of wakefulness don't let you
come to easily.

SUNDAY, JULY 13

A need to see the sun; I went out after noon; my first walk since I got
sick. Anaphiotika, the Acropolis, the trees on the Areopagus, the grove
of Philopappus. Light strong and pure, revealing everything with such
astonishing clarity that I had the serious feeling of a sudden hallucination
in broad daylight. Returning, as I was looking at the north side of the
Acropolis, rocks and marble together with the Byzantine chapel below—
just as one discerns faces and shapes on an old wall—I saw the tall skeleton
of a woman, bones snow-white, looking at me with a proud air like the
ghost of a hero. She looked from a world that was no longer of today,
but a future world where nothing of what I know, things or persons, had
survived. I felt the same love that I have now for life with all its beauties
and evils—exactly the same love for this snow-white skeleton in the sun.
These are strange things I've written and yet it was that way. I can't
express it more precisely. I have the impression that I saw a moment of
eternity.

MONDAY, JULY 14

I started regular work at the Ministry again. In the fall the operation, and after the hospital—to Ankara.

SATURDAY, JULY 19

At Grandpa's, in Psychiko. He had a reception for some Americans, mostly clergymen. A few ancient ladies, indomitable hags, MacVeagh, and the Ecumenical Patriarch, whom I met for the first time. You could feel the boredom that emanates from this man, like mist. In his glance are countless dark rooms, narrow alleys, compressed and bruised souls.

I wonder if the concrete image of the blind poet (in the poem about Homer) was suggested to Solomos by the beggar Kokondris.

WEDNESDAY, JULY 23

This morning after a conference at the Ministry of Coordination, I heard the instruments of the secret troupe. The hour has come. I remembered Henry Miller when he was leaving Greece; it was so painful for him when he made the decision. "Now I no longer care," he said, "I've felt the finger of Destiny." Last night at Varymbobi, Spon said: "When a country prevents you from thinking logically, you must abandon it." He, too, was bidding us goodbye. With people, with cities, that's how it goes.

FRIDAY, AUGUST 1

Touti gave birth to two snow white kittens: her negatives.

WEDNESDAY, AUGUST 6

Last night, outside Zappeion, we met Sikelianos. We sat with him a while at the small café near the entrance. I asked about his health. "Yes, I do have high blood pressure," he answered, "but it's Sikelianos' high blood pressure!" It is not he who fits into the world's measurements; the world fits into his measurements.

SATURDAY, AUGUST 9

When all is said, the moment comes when you realize that the machine of transubstantiation runs in reverse, returning whatever is unique, whatever has flourished, to the state of the seed that follows other seeds through the millstones.

MONDAY, AUGUST 11

Looking at the topic (cultural civilization) I have to delve into tomorrow at the Ministry I observe: (a) That Greek critical thought throughout the nineteenth century has been devoured for the most part by the language question. (b) That the beginning of the trend toward the study of the folk tradition (I mean Athens, not the Heptanesian School) is due to Fallmerayer's attack. And even N.C. Politis sets out to prove that we have preserved the customs of the ancient Greeks. (c) That all the major poets of Greece were accused of being "cerebral," regardless of whether the critics used this epithet. Thus with Solomos (see Zambelios), Palamas, Cavafy. (d) That every new movement has been accused of decadence; see, e.g., Angelos Vlachos' attack upon the naturalism of Zola, Flaubert, and Daudet.

Marvelous! We found Theophilos and Makriyannis, in the way that nymphomaniac tourists find shepherd boys to make love to them: primitivism in reverse. And those people have found this piece of candy and keep on chewing it, with pleasure. But the problem is that in our poor Greece I do not find any of our academic painters, the devil take me, who have the color and the air of Theophilos, and when I pick up one page from Makriyannis' Memoirs and a page from the Memoirs of Rangavis, an amazingly educated man for his time, I find after all, that the word, the phrase, the tone, the rhythm, the literary text of the scholarly man seems like nonsense beside the writing of the illiterate.*

*Makriyannis (1797–1864), an illiterate general in the Greek War of Independence who taught himself the Greek alphabet in order to write his Memoirs. Seferis, who called him "my master," wrote an important essay on him in 1943. An abridged version of the Memoirs has been translated into English by H. A. Lidderdale (Oxford University Press, 1966).

And lest it be thought that I am prejudiced by the difference between the demotic and katharevousa, I would add that, to me, even Rangavis' thinking seems sinewless and sparkless beside the naive thinking of Makriyannis. This is the Greek phenomenon, the Greek problem, which one must consider coldly.

SUNDAY, AUGUST 17

Since Friday, the Feast of the Virgin, in Kifissia, at Polemon's. We returned this evening. They love us and we love them, but they live in another world, with a nervous, unstable morbidity in its atmosphere.

Looking through a ground floor window at a palm tree (I don't understand the association; we didn't have a palm tree at that house), I remembered the summer of 1926 with my mother.

Very slowly I cast off the stern line. The fullness of time has come.

TUESDAY, AUGUST 26

Terribly hot both on the streets and at home. You don't know what to do. Work impossible. And the hospital ahead of me. A miserable way of life and waste of time. Feeling of a prison.

SUNDAY, AUGUST 31

The XAN Camp, Phaneromeni, Salamis.* Here since yesterday with G. Apostolidis. We set out around 9 from Athens. In the afternoon Koulouri, Moulki, the St. Nicholas monastery, and a late return.

Moulki is full of old churches, you meet them at every step, movingly beautiful. In the village the Dormition of the Virgin; unfortunately, the icons are wretchedly modern: Jesus on the waters steps on a pulp of murky yogurt. Farther down at St. John, near the spring, something of the old frescoes has survived. On the right, the Saint (I suppose), superb

*Christian Brotherhood of Young Men.

face, and a Virgin on the left. The first really beautiful one. Still farther, St. Sotera. On the left side something still remains: a table with a fish in the middle; table objects like Tsarouhis' "still lifes." To St. Nicholas by mule, about an hour's climb. The monastery is now occupied by nuns; cypress trees, a graceful palm tree. On the left (facing the sea), beyond a spring enveloped in a cloud of wasps, St. John's Chapel. All these chapels have a graceful architecture, except St. Nicholas, which is something else, with pointed arches (Frankish?). Beyond, the sea with islands and dancing mountain peaks. It had grown dark while we were climbing down; the moon, though full, couldn't light our way through the ravine.

From Moulki we took with us in the jeep a native who begged a ride. We asked him if we'd find a place to eat. "Go to so-and-so's," he told us, "not to so-and-so's; at so-and-so's you'll even see Takoue dancing. She comes when the moon is full. There are no fish then and the fishermen spend the night at Koulouri. She leaves with the waning moon. Since before the war she has pocketed all their money. Now she's old; she's thirty-five, but she still dances beautifully."

At Koulouri we found neither Takoue nor anything to eat. In front of our tent the channel with full moon—awe-inspiring. I'm unhappy.

MONDAY, SEPTEMBER 1, ATHENS

Government crisis for a week now. The wheel has turned many times since the era of Hector MacNeil. Poor Damaskinos.*

MONDAY, SEPTEMBER 8

This story is becoming very expensive; you have to buy stacks of newspapers. K. has collected volumes of clippings. After the wrangle over the dreadful clique, Athens has been in an uproar for days now about the Domaine Grec.* The story of the pumpkin game; why is it four and

*Damaskinos (1890–1949), Archbishop of Athens, served as Regent in the years 1944–1946, and Prime Minister for a short time in 1945.
*Robert Levesque, Domaine Grec, 1939–1946 (Genèva–Paris, 1947).

not five, why you and not me? The cause is a foolish phrase of Robert Levesque, whose book is, nevertheless, a hymn to Greece. But this man would prefer blowing up the Eiffel Tower to sacrificing a phrase he considers just right. Once he wrote of me as "Consul." But I wasn't a "Consul," I observed. And, when I persuaded him to replace the word: "Dommage, ça sonnait bien mieux."

SEPTEMBER 12

Yesterday at the Herod Atticus Theater; Agamemnon by the Students' Group of the Sorbonne. This performance moves you and makes you think.

MONDAY, SEPTEMBER 15

Yesterday to Epidaurus (by boat) to see the Persians, again by the students. Wretched organizing: donkey braying behind Darius' ghost. The machine for the Martenot waves had been broken in transport. The kids tried their best. Aeschylus interests me so much that I didn't pay attention to whether or not they succeeded. The theater: that's the most important character in the drama.

On Saturday, at Demangel's dinner, I met Axel Persson, who did the excavations at Asine. I felt an affinity for him.

WEDNESDAY, SEPTEMBER 17

Since the beginning of the month our bedroom has resembled a house under construction. We live and sleep in the study in a shambles of dust, furniture, and our three kittens. Yesterday, again to Aeschylus at the Herod Atticus Theater. We bought cheap tickets and climbed up high. I enjoyed the performance, sitting on the ground to watch.

THURSDAY, OCTOBER 16

Dr. Kairis gave me a ticket for Evangelismos Hospital. Who knows what the performance will be.

SATURDAY, OCTOBER 25

In September the house was a construction site; in October dismantled bookcases, crates, and packing for the trip to Ankara. Fortunately the pressure of putting things in order was absorbing enough so that the hospital day came without my thinking much about it. I came and moored like a ship whose timetable I knew, but which was not bringing me any specially loved person.

Tired and disgusted, I took the ticket the doctor gave me, like a ticket for vacation, and came to this establishment. Rest: here I'm nothing but number 212; I have no personality; I participate in the common personality of suffering men. My room is characterless, it has a geometric shape, long and narrow like a corridor. But it faces the street, and at night the lights of the houses are like harbor lights.

I started reading (I haven't read for weeks) the books I picked up at random when I left hurriedly—by chance, Virginia Woolf's "On Not Knowing Greek," among others. For the first time in a long while everything amuses me; I'm in that mood again. It would be better if the toilets were cleaner. One of them doesn't even have water. That stench gives the hospital the character of a latrine. Nonetheless, the enema is called hypoenema.

SUNDAY, OCTOBER 26

Hospital mass production; the misery of human bodies under repair. You must see it first hand in order to understand the elation and catharsis of the ritual of love.

I must take carbon for tomorrow's X-ray. The nurse who brings me a cup of black juice tells me to take a spoonful every hour. I persuade her to let me take three spoonfuls every quarter of an hour. I calculate that with the original instructions I would need at least twenty hours to empty

the cup. Too bad: it was relaxing to obey without responsibility; now I
realize I must analyze the orders.

TUESDAY, OCTOBER 28

Last year at this time I was on Poros cutting wood, swimming, and
writing. No matter: "Tomorrow brings a new day." Daybreak on
Hymettus, seen from my window, reminds me of the dawn of the 28th in
1940 more than any other time.* Almost the same landscape as from
the Ministry of Foreign Affairs at 4 A.M., almost the same mood of
anticipation.

Yesterday and today I've been concentrating on what bothers me here. It
isn't the poor facilities, the hole-riddled blankets, celluloid dishes, worn-
out silverware, cold food, etc.—our country's suffering from the war has
been inconceivable. What can we do?—but deficiencies resulting from
laziness, indifference, bad management: e.g., dull needles for syringes,
broken tubes, etc. Yesterday they took me downstairs for X-rays; all the
patients, without exception, out-patient and in-patient, lie on the same
board, naked on the wood, with the same pillow, without any intervening
cleansing or putting of a clean sheet down between. Worse, for three
days now I've been trying to find a way to wash myself a little. The
faces of the staff give the impression that you're asking for something
inordinately absurd. Yesterday I finally managed to get them to give me a
basin of hot water in an unspeakably filthy bathroom; an entire village
defecates there. You tell this to the nurse, to this one, to that one. "There
are so many patients," they reply; "they're not careful." Agreed. But
when you tell them the water isn't running, they pretend not to hear.
And just think that with the cost of five days for one patient they could
clean, repair, and paint all these sections in my ward, not counting
UNRRA and three years of reconstruction.

Such a large institution is somewhat like a holy city: Jerusalem, Delphi—

*The Italian invasion in Greece on October 28, 1940.

superstitution and moneymaking. I don't mean the doctors and the nurses; most of them are excellent people, often touching; I mean a lower stratum.

WEDNESDAY, OCTOBER 29

A bright day, a day for a beginning. Through my window, which I left wide open, an unrestrained intoxication rushes into the narrow room and abolishes consciousness.

Tomorrow morning I'm to be operated on. The anticipation is no more disagreeable than other ordinary anticipations of life's petty miseries. The dominant feeling within me is, I think, curiosity.

THURSDAY, OCTOBER 30, HALF-PAST MIDNIGHT

I woke up; I don't know if it was from nervousness. It seems rather from the drugs they gave me. I heard the trolley, I looked at the shutters, I thought it was dawn; lucky for me, I slept—I thought. I turned on the light; it was 12. Outside in Athens, a bright moon; I had the feeling of the condemned man's last night. Then, suddenly, absolute calm. Fine.

Morning. I had finished shaving and was waiting for them to come and take me to the operating room, when the assistant came in—with a fever himself—to tell me that Dr. Kairis had had a terrible reaction from the cholera vaccine given the hospital personnel yesterday, that he had to stay in bed, and that the operation wouldn't take place. Disappointment, then, a feeling somewhat of the ridiculous: as when you see someone making heroic gestures and suddenly realize that all these are completely meaningless. Occasional boredom throughout the day with the thought that the new anticipation will be the same as the old—to no avail.

SATURDAY, NOVEMBER 1

Incredible how many ship images the hospital creates—the uniform food, the austere appearance of the doctors, almost militaristic as they enter with their staff; the people you half-see in bed as if they were seasick; the feeling that you have embarked without being able to leave until you arrive at a terminus, at a port.

MONDAY, NOVEMBER 10

(Dictated to Maró.) Today was a better day. In the morning they removed two bandages from the wound. Though as of tomorrow eight days will have passed since the operation, I still sleep poorly. It's questionable whether I sleep more than three hours day and night. The day begins to be very tiring, unbearable. As it starts growing dark, the constriction in my breathing does not diminish. I must have inhaled an enormous amount of ether last Tuesday. They described scenes of inconceivably foul language and wrestling as I was coming out of anesthesia. I still have black and blue marks on my skin from the latter.

What I observe with much more interest than all this is my window. It shows a very common square of light, a patch of slope on Hymettus— three or four hand-spans of earth—a narrow pine-covered area, and in the foreground, walls and houses from the neighborhood opposite. And yet these trivial things in this light acquire such an astonishing intensity of life that even these days, when I'm nothing more than a shipwreck tossing in the midst of free associations, this square of light can hold my attention; it keeps me above the surface as if I were a healthy man.

This morning a letter from Rex. He's leaving for Germany and wants to know about my health. He recalls that a year ago I was writing the "Thrush" on Poros. He longs for Greece. I would like to write him, if I could, about the feelings this corner of the window invokes in me; it is not the corner of the view of a tranquil countryside—it would be very natural then—but, instead, the view through a window of a deeply wounded man. I mean to say that it isn't at all the beauty of the land- scape, or the restfulness of vacation, or the idyllic atmosphere of an island that makes the difference, but the existence of this light, even upon trivial objects, its very existence, even seen through the filthy windowpanes of the Evangelismos.

FRIDAY, NOVEMBER 14

I ate chicken. Sikelianos came and presented me with two roses, the most beautiful I've ever seen. And he knows how to offer them.

SATURDAY, NOVEMBER 29

At about 11 A.M. I came back home. Without awareness. I now understand bit by bit, through silent echoes that rise to the surface, the change of climate, the horror of the hospital: the smells, the noises, and the unbearable boredom of the rhythm of recovery.

WEDNESDAY, DECEMBER 10

The day before yesterday I went out for the first time: a quarter of an hour at the Zappeion.

When all is said and done, this remains: that nothing else exists but this oil lamp—life, nothing else.

WEDNESDAY, DECEMBER 31

23:45 o'clock. I finished the manuscript for the second edition of my Eliot translations. I started working on it at home to pass the hours of convalescence. I'm not supposed to move too much, and my mind was working sluggishly. I thought it would be a mechanical job. At times it was more than that.

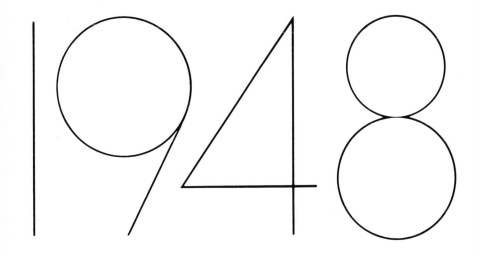

SUNDAY, JANUARY 5

My wound closed yesterday. Today, to the Ministry. Sometimes men are so indifferent that you have the urge, as your eye falls on the inkwell on their desks, to empty it over their heads and wake them up.

SATURDAY, JANUARY 17

Late in the afternoon Grandpa asked me to go to Psychiko; he was expecting Eden, passing through Athens after a tour of the Middle East. This Englishman talks to him affectionately. Conversation: melancholy generalities. I accompanied him to the door below. Before he said goodbye, he brought his palms together, raised them to the sky, and sighed: "Humanity! . . . Humanity!" It seemed to me that he was suddenly on stage, and I was watching him.

SUNDAY, JANUARY 25

We turned the house on Kydathenaion Street over to the American woman tenant and moved to Kifissia, to Maris K.'s.

WEDNESDAY, FEBRUARY 4, MORNING, S.S. ISTANBUL

Throughout January rushing around and excitement for the trip. Physical resistance weakening; it's a nuisance to be obliged (for the first time) to gauge your strength. The last days in Kifissia were a gift of God, but last night on board ship was the first time I've slept without any worry.

The thought of Ankara depressed me. Now I feel more lighthearted; I think I prefer anything to the confinement of Athens—the mental, I mean. In the Ministry, total incarceration; in literature, the threat that if you speak your mind openly you'll be accused of expressing the ideas of others. And the wretched feeling of seeing the language shriveling, becoming a conventional stammer, because of fanaticism.

The volley of insults against me has become fashionable of late, yet never have I parted from Athens in such an atmosphere of friendship. A touching warmth, often unexpected: the evening at the Athenaion, last Friday, was very spirited—so many unknown friends, mostly young.

One must get away.

The other night at Kifissia a raging wind and cloudburst. In the morning I went to say goodbye to Sikelianos. He came down to the hotel lobby somewhat tired; he doesn't like appearing this way. "Gandhi's death has depressed me," he said. I rarely realize how deeply this man's perception reaches. Will we ever meet again?

The Sea of Marmara is calm beneath the morning sun. I feel a little like an unstrung violin in its case. Only Turkish is spoken around me; even the stewards don't know three Christian words.

SUNDAY, MARCH 21

Still (since our arrival) at the Park Oteli. It's difficult to find a house in Ankara. For weeks now (since we arrived) I've been moving in a haze. Sickness reduces us to purely elemental functions. Last night was the Persian New Year; in the "acemce" embassy, as the taxi drivers call it, a voracious mob in tailcoats. At midnight I couldn't stand on my feet any longer. I don't know why I feel so heavily tired here; as soon as it grows dark, I become leaden. I thought it was the aftereffects of the hospital, of migration, and of that dreadful reconstructed Athens. I don't know; it must be something to do with the climate; I can't breathe enough on this utterly barren plateau, without a notion of green; you would think I'd entered the kingdom of sleep.

On top of all this, the other sickness. The drama of the place and the humiliation of men between the Clashing Rocks of this third world war.* Once the heimatlos was the man without a country; today it's the man without a party.

MONDAY, APRIL 12

Worse and worse all the time: I'm like a bag of chaff which is carried around. As the sun sets I can't bear it any longer; I drag myself to the hotel, eat something, and lie down; sleep is a bedsheet of birdlime. The doctor I saw—a German Jew exiled since the time of Hitler—a sympathetic man, told me: "Vous n'êtes pas intéressant comme malade, c'est la radio-activité de la steppe . . ." I replied, "Radioactivité? c'est aussi mystérieux que l'existence de Dieu." The trouble is that the radioactivity of this steppe makes you uninteresting as a person too.

MONDAY, APRIL 19

I mailed young Valaoritis my contribution to the book commemorating

*The Clashing Rocks (Symplegades), two legendary rocks or islands at the entrance of the Black Sea, which crushed any ship that tried to pass between them.

Eliot's sixtieth birthday. The text was written almost without any books, at a little table with hardly room enough for my elbows; this hotel life is prolonged unbearably.

MAY

Great fuss about Solomos in Athens. From what has reached me down here: words, words. I have a great desire to write an essay with the title: "Have mercy on Solomos."

TUESDAY, JUNE 15

Flowering of chest and thighs on the sand—

Mr. Praxias, the party leader, preaches, "let's cleanse the Augean stables of collaborationism." Of course the collaborators, who are his own men and whom he supports, are not collaborators as far as he is concerned.

FRIDAY, JUNE

I know they would like me to write what is like them, just as Ethiopian iconographers paint the Holy Virgins black.

To the appropriate office to get a driver's license. A common man hears me speaking Greek, approaches, and impulsively bursts into tears with all the passion of his soul. A Cretan Turk: "Eh well, what can they understand, here in the depths of Anatolia, about our island? Such an island . . ." I felt deep sympathy for this uprooted man.

In between the cornerstones of the Castle a marble key design sometimes meanders like a lizard peering forth.

SUNDAY, JUNE 20

"Professor Logre described an illness characterized 'by the incomplete awaking from sleep with transitory memory disturbances' leading to accidents wrongly attributed until today by the courts and even by doctors to the patient's environment. He called this illness 'La syndrome d'Elpénor,' for Homer already has described 'with astonishing preciseness of observation' a case of this illness in the Odyssey when Odysseus describes the fatal accident that befell Elpenor, one of his companions, during his stay with Circe" (sic, from Kathimerini, June 7).

Elpenor's syndrome. Well, we must be careful what we write; who knows, maybe someday it will become an illness officially.

THURSDAY, JULY 1

We moved from the Park Oteli to Boulevard Ataturk 373. We have a home finally! Last Easter morning, in the loneliness of the hotel, with the office red pencil I colored two eggs for good luck. We had no other way of saying "Christ Has Risen."

AUGUST

Departing, returning, departing, returning, in the end
every twig, every oar, every seashore is blood-stained
and you hear nothing but the howls of Scylla.
I am with you, friend and enemy,
shouts a cripple.
Wait, I am with you . . .

Flowers and leaves caught in the quiet light—

And the poet shut up in a small house, with icons
seeking windows behind their frames—

And the moon dressed in linen with the arched wings of a dove—
(see Homeric Hymn to Selene, l. 1: τανυσίπτερος)*

---

*Τανυσίπτερος = with extended wings, long-winged.

SEPTEMBER 2

Yesterday's bulletin of the East News Agency: "Karl Arnold a affirmé au Conseil Parlementaire de l'Allemagne à Bonn qu' Hitler n'était pas une apparition spécifiquement allemande mais la personnification du nihilisme européen." Similarly, one evening at Koritsa, I heard it announced on the radio that the German people are free of original sin! Their lack of conscience is irredeemable.

SEPTEMBER 6

I mailed—the "Diary of a poem."

OCTOBER 8

Oedipean

Sherlock Holmes has branch offices everywhere
all over the earth, all over the world;
Oedipus interrogates the shepherd everywhere
without knowing what lies in wait for him.

At the crossroads dead Laius lies in ambush
and in the gardens you hear murmers: "blind in the ears . . . "*
Time runs, nervous, with a broken-down brake,
Sir! here eyes and lights are extinguished!

These days I have been reading the Explanation of the Art of Painting
by Dionysius of Fourna which I borrowed in Constantinople (Petrograd,
1900): "A house, and Christ seated at the table with Simon and the
Apostles, and the whore behind Christ holding a broken glass jug over his
head" (§76).

Characteristic: he pays special attention to the beard, together with
other details—flesh, hair, garments; see, e.g., "The Greek sages who
spoke about the incarnate economy of Christ" (§130): Apollonius has

*Sophocles, Oedipus the King, I. 371.

"a long, forked beard"; Thucydides "a tripartite beard"; Solon "a round beard"; Plutarch "a pointed beard"; Sophocles is "bald, with a beard parted in fifths"; Plato, "a long, wide beard." Somewhere else there's someone with a "bulrush beard."

In Byzantine art everything is traditional, predetermined by tradition (see also about the copying of designs)*; it is a "god-given" art (from Fourna); it issues from the Sacred Scarf, the icons are miraculous because they are god-given; its basis is imitation. And yet, in spite of what people say, it has lived, with intermittent reflowering, for so many centuries. In this art the excellent artist excels by a minute deviation from the traditional; it is entirely the opposite of our violent changes, every so often; for better or worse, I don't know. The ultimate evil of the Byzantines is ossification; the ultimate evil for us is dissolution. However, some day I would like to ask Tsarouhis to make me an icon of Jonah inscribed, "I have been grieving deeply over the gourd nigh unto death" (see instructions in § 119). Most of our griefs are for gourds.

OCTOBER

In the garden yellow leaves and charcoal—

Just as when
the whore who holds a bottle
full of stifling scent,
and the glass breaks,
and the spilled myrrh lingers for days,
so murder has spread over our skins
and does not peel off—

OCTOBER

"Noon came, and the Old Man emerged from the sea, and found the seals.
We seized him; he had forgotten none of his tricks;
he turned into a shaggy lion,

*Byzantine iconographers used earlier icons or frescoes as their models and often traced them.

then a dragon and a leopard,
into a huge boar,
into flowing water,
into a tree whose top is thick with leaves.
Our hands held him fast.
When he exhausted his magic spells and grew weary
he told me and asked me . . . ''

(δ 450 ff.)

"But to the Elysian fields, to the bounds of the earth
the immortals will send you, where golden-haired Rhadamanthus dwells,
where the good life awaits men.
Neither snow, nor heavy winter, nor even rain
but always the sweet breaths of the West Wind
come from the Ocean and refresh men.''
He spoke and plunged into the waves of the sea.

(δ 563 ff.)*

I'm thinking of Hesiod speaking about Ionia.

NOVEMBER

    (Argo)

I've learned my fairytales on ships,
not from travelers or sailors
or from the others waiting on the docks,
forever ashore, searching their pockets for cigarettes.
Faces of ships inhabit my life;
some stare one-eyed like the Cyclops,
motionless in the mirror of the sea,
some behave like the ant, some like the butterfly,
some move like sleepwalkers, dangerously,

*Homer, The Odyssey, bk. IV, ll. 450–461, 563–570.

and some are taken by the sleep of the depths—
timbers, ropes, sails, chains, and all.
In the cool little house in the garden,
under the acacias and the eucalyptuses,
near the rusted windmill,
near the yellow cistern with a single goldfish
in the cool little house smelling of osier,
I found a ship's compass
that showed me the heralds of the winds—

SUNDAY

A few days ago, as I was thinking about last year in Athens, I saw a pack of
mad dogs attacking me.

WEDNESDAY

For days now in bed with pains; x-rays and so on.

CHRISTMAS

I've just read this tale by Ruskin: "Turner was once sketching some ships
a mile or two from Plymouth Harbor, with the setting sun behind them.
He showed his sketch to a naval officer. The officer observed that the
ships did not have portholes. "No," said the artist; "from this distance
and in this light, you cannot make out portholes." "True," said the
officer, "but you know that the ships do have portholes." "Correct," said
Turner, "but my job is to paint what I see, not what I know." (Proust
mentions it in Pastiches et mélanges, p. 172.)

How many people do ask for portholes in places where no one sees them;
because they know them.

> In the Night

The smokeless glow of the silver torch
recalls me from the seventh world of sleep.

The pine tree on my wall is a shadow, growing.
On my window's blank paper
the brush is a shadow drawing the shadow of a hill.
In my room, tonight, life is a shadow.
I know not if I am awake or still asleep; the breath of music
in the silence may be the wind
playing with the pine's ghost, or is it a song
issuing from a hidden stringless lyre?

(Tsoi Tsung, Korea, 2nd century)

MONDAY, DECEMBER

The year is ending. The embassies of Ankara are always at a standstill,
like buoys permanently anchored to the snow-covered steppe; every two
or three weeks, a mailman may come and bring them nourishing supplies
of news for the next period; then, absolute silence.

JANUARY

The snow here is endless. In Attica
it is received like an interval of relief
or with a veneration presaging the almond trees
or Karaghiozis' screen when the bagpipes cease.
The people rejoice; they go off to the countryside and forget
misery. The snow here
is a zero. Miles below zero,
with the glitter of white sand, faces
without cheeks, without shape, eyes
staring, without the blessed earth.
I should not dare speak of prayers, yet
sometimes they slay a lamb for sacrifice,
blood spurts like a blinding explosion of the sun—

At moments everything departs, and every sound,
as if heard for the first time, falls, you think,
onto a palm of marble or wood.
And men depart and give birth to statues—

Sinking into dreams of fruits and leaves,
gardens with nude trunks and moist lips—

TUESDAY, APRIL 26. ON THE TRAIN TO CONSTANTINOPLE

Bones whiten on the empty plains of Anatolia,
and frogs spread scaly sounds in the night;
like a city's vanished currency that reappears to show us suddenly the
   circulation of gain and loss, passions that blazed and dried up—

THURSDAY, APRIL 28, BURSA

We left by boat for Bursa at 9:00; Mudanya at 13:00.

A fountain by the seashore; a ditch under pomegranate trees; pomegranates in the light of the setting sun, reeds and voices of children.

The water glides in the shade, shines in the sun; the water runs, whispers;
love returns. In the country everyone is weaving; the sound of looms as you
pass. Poplars; the valley buried many brave men—

SUNDAY, MAY DAY

Olympus of Bithynia, its monks belonging to another time. The foliage
of music: how music builds a nest; how it strengthens its foliage.

   Alla Marcia

Beating the brine, day and night,
no one altered destiny;
beating the darkness and the light,
no one altered murder.

But the light may be reborn;
the seeds can once more fall
upon the heavy palms.
Blood can flower again.

BRUSA, 5 IN THE MORNING

Canzona

Figure of sunken sanctuaries,
mother of ignorance and wisdom,
mother of strife and of peace,
land of the living.

By singing fountains,
where the waters were unleashed,
by the sound of the loom,
where the snow is endless,
when we grieve and when we rejoice
over important things and over the gourd,*
help us.

Above the bright gloom of the desert
and among the nations that love
or hate or ignore us;
in cities shriveled within their walls;
down in the plains of the enemies,
stand by us.

And among our brothers spinning
the two-branched blood in their veins,
in the wild fear of love,
in the tenderness of hate,
in the downhill of darkness,
help us.

*See Jonah, IV.—G. S.

Allow us sleep with dreams
like our oars, like the dreams
embroidered on our skins
with the patience of the sea;
not Ephialtes the juggler.

MONDAY, MAY 9

Tomorrow we leave for Ankara.

Intimacy with the sea, with love, with death.
Love upright like the flame.

"Ratto, ratto, che'l tempo non si perda
per poco amor . . . "

(Purgatorio, 18, 103)

FRIDAY, MAY 13, ANKARA

Cocteau's Machine infernale. After so many years I found the play
boring, shallow, and aged. It didn't move me at all, except for the catastrophe scene—which isn't his; you hang onto it like an anchorline and
head toward the ancient tragedy. Alas, inevitably you are let down in the
last scene—the scene of the Frankish Madonna, I called it—where Jocasta's
ghost appears; there nothing can help you any longer.

I heard him talking yesterday in the University auditorium. Incredible what
flatteries he contrived to line up and what cheap compliments. The
audience led him on. Listen—Ankara: "sortie comme Minerve de la tête de
Jupiter!" (Jupiter = Kemal). Kemal: "lumineux, illuminé, illuminant!"
The Turks: "qui pensent avant d'agir, tandisque les Français agissent avant
de penser!" (See Valéry, about Mallarmé, I think.) Talking about Gide in
a charitable tone, unbearably petty. "Who knows for what petty motives
he wrote the Marche Turque? Let's not bother with him; Gide did the
same to him."

MONDAY, MAY 16

Last night Ram Gopal—Indian dances. I recalled Uday Shankar, one of the strongest impressions of my London years, and I went with warm sympathy: disappointment. Where I expected an art like the one I had known at that time, I found mass-produced pantomime, degenerate, dull, and exhibitionist. Compared with the remembrance of young Shankar, the man here appeared heavy, plump, graceless. And the magic, the ritualistic tone of the music, had been lost. I returned home sadly.

FRIDAY, MAY 20

"Grandpa" has died; with all his good and bad traits, he was a strong man, genuine. His last message: "Many happy returns on St. George's Day."

SATURDAY, JUNE 4

Fifteen days ago I renewed the cleaning up and copying of the diary from 1925 until the end of '47. Now it's the only way to apply some discipline to myself. I feel so miserable, so out-of-breath here I've concluded that only an engine could start me up. I turned this engine on last winter. Miserable months: endless snowfall that became a nightmare, unbearable pain (a month in bed), and extreme bitterness because of my friends. I recorded in a fresh notebook about fifty pages from 1938–39; it tired me more than if I had written a book.

"Second- or third-rate" work. However, even in the past, in much livelier times, it often occurred to me that some day I had to decide to do it or else burn these notebooks. I didn't yield to this negativism; I don't like to renounce myself or hide; I don't think one can get anywhere through rejection.

Now that I'm copying and, I can say, reading for the first time, right from the beginning, these lines which I wrote as circumstances dictated, I note that the question is not one of confessions nor of stressing the most important things. Maybe the diary partakes of all these, just as I myself partake in whatever I am doing. But it has no aspiration toward completeness. At most it is the footprints one leaves as he passes by. "The footprints on the snow," to recall that music of Claude-Achille [Debussy]; footprints from a few moments, not always the most important but the most convenient; those that happened along. So there are many and great gaps—

Telephone; I must go; I haven't time enough to complete my thought.

SUNDAY, JUNE 5

I never imagined this return to the diary would be so painful; written only to keep the habit of the pen (mainly in the most depressing years of my public service) and also in order to remember my teachers.

EVENING

In my youth I had a tendency to jot down moments of distress. Perhaps it's progress: I now feel sorry when I note that the expansion of joy didn't impel me as easily toward paper.

JUNE

The evil
in our blood, in our kidneys, in our wakefulness,
in our hunger, in our thirst, in our exhaustion—

Nurses with enormous eyes,
the anesthetist and the surgeon,
and the curtains of pain,
and the superstition about the hospital,
and the expectation of the scalpel,
in the early dawn elevator.

And the coming out of the ether building
like a drunk out of a brothel—

SUNDAY, JULY 24

Excursion! We went with Annoula and took a dip in a pool about twenty-five kilometers outside of Ankara. At night I felt such a longing for the sea, such an ineffable longing.

    Elpenor:

Down here I now know
Hades and Dionysus are the same

wasting a long time in order to die

Last night I started reading the first volume of Palamas' Poetics. I fell asleep when I had finished the Foreword and Chatzopoulos' review of Vomous. Heavy, pulpy prose, yet one must admit that Palamas is certainly the best critical mind we have had. Chatzopoulos' prose is worse and unbearably bastardized by journalistic admixtures. It is a subject for serious study, this inability of our poets to express themselves in prose. Look at Sikelianos; Malakasis couldn't even jot a line of prose. Offhand one could say "their wings prevent them from walking"; but why are they always entangled in their wings? Solomos didn't lack wings; yet he's a first-rate prose writer. While in the others inspiration makes even their walking roll and pitch. Sometimes the literary language clearly weighs them down, bad habits, bad tradition; they remain, even in their demotic, pedants. The subject is interesting; I would look at it from another point of view. They learned poetry only from the poetry they had at their disposal, and if prose existed, they considered it anti-poetic to benefit from it; for poetic purposes, I mean. It would be very useful if our poets learned to use prose for poetic purposes. Language at its root is a unified thing. I mean here the rhythms of language, too, not excepting any good text, not even conversation. Anyhow, after what happened yesterday, I read a few lines of Makriyannis this morning: a purgatorial bath.

MONDAY, AUGUST 1

"L'Angolo Franciscano"

Between the days of the cherry and the days of the wild cherry,
when the apricots begin to ripen
and you do not hear the apples fall,
the small garden with no horizon
and everywhere the leaves hold hands and hem you in.
Among these mountains with color beyond life,
in these wildernesses, dry depths
from seas you might once have sailed,
in the small garden, here, the fruits,
here, the children of religion;
unripe offerings ripe offerings rotten offerings.
"How did we become like this?"
Better to ask
the wizards the jugglers and the villains,
for me it is enough
to look at this foliage, this body;
unripe corners ripe corners beaten corners.
The cherries have gone by the apples will be late
and the moon with arched dove wings,
dressed in linen,
as I hear in the small cistern the endless dripping,
rosary of a novice, beads from a cheap fair—
and the whore holding the broken glass of myrrh
down by the willows of Sodom.

FRIDAY, AUGUST 5

Ankara Monument

Once a month, once every three weeks,
messengers come, messengers go.
What decree has sent them nobody knows;
neither the old men with their stork bones

nor the maidens with brows like swallows' wings
nor even the dry mountains in Gallo-Graecia.
They come from the East and they come from the West,
from the North and from the South, roses of the wind.
They let loose the stallions and run to get drunk,
and they leave the tavernas reeling, and go
raving obscenely, crazed and visionary.
One speaks of Augustus who had castles for scales,
another looks for Holy Virgins who pined in caves,
and still another, low of brow, seeks King Asitawandas,
whose father was the storm, whose mother the tempest,
who now is left speechless like a dried-up river.
But Stathis the monk who exhausted himself roaming
and was once a swordbearer, swordbearer and hangman,
sits at the fountain, the blindness bringing water,
stares into the sunset, speaks, and relates:
"Unto the world below you sent me, my Lord and Christ,
and bodily I departed and bodily I went;
now I seek your grace, guardian of sin;
seed of Charon I sowed, for others to reap,
yet make me sprout for you from my grave
a carnation of my lament and come to your side."

AUGUST

A few days ago Mr. M. gave me the text of the Hittite inscription of
Karatepe as it has been deciphered recently. I had asked for it: I'm
translating from the English:

Truly I am Asitawandas, man of the Sun, servant of the God of Storm.
Awarku, King of Andanawa, nurtured me.
The God of Storm made me mother and father of the city of Andanawa.
I have revived the city of Andanawa.
And I have spread the plain of Andanawa to the West and to the East.

The expressionless statues of the Hittites left me cold. These inarticulate people were practically nonexistent for me, but now I have heard their halting speech, I think about them.

THURSDAY, AUGUST 18

News from California: Otis Berton's bathyscaph reached 1370 meters. "Nombreux poissons rencontrés dans les grands fonds dont la luminosité était-aveuglante . . . Il se plaignait du froid intense qui régnait dans le benthoscope." It seems to me that when we say we love the sea, it is the epidermis of the sea that we love.

MONDAY, AUGUST 22

Epitaph For My Cat Touti Who Passed Away Last Fall

She had the color of ebony, the eyes of Salome,
Touti, the cat that I lost; passerby, do not stop.
She rose from the chasm that ripped the sheet of day,
now she cannot tear the cloth of darkness.

SUNDAY, AUGUST 28

I'm reading Gide's foreword to the Anthology of French Poetry (Pléiade), a melancholy foreword, written before the War, with a postscript in April 1947. It doesn't at all resemble the image of Gide which we had been accustomed to until now. Not that he isn't right when he speaks about the oblivion of our works and the "return of chaos"; but one is startled that he has only now discovered these things. I preferred the liveliness one felt behind that "J'ai vécu" of his Theseus. He writes: "Tout cela (le système poétique de naguère) n'a plus raison d'être dès l'instant que l'instant seul compte et qu'il n'y a plus d'avenir. J'écrivais, avant la guerre: 'Je ne gagnerai mon procès qu'en appel,' ou 'J'écris pour être relu'—et cela ne signifie plus rien, du moment qu'il n'y a plus d'appel et qu'il n'est plus question de relire." Melancholy, autumnal phrases; sad his discouragement. We are going through difficult, transient times. With our experience, who of us believes his works will live forever?

This feeling is not new. We felt it during the interwar years; it doesn't surprise us that it is now more intense; it will not surprise us if the situation worsens. We have accepted the fact that we will be forgotten. —"Who will weigh for us this decision of oblivion?"* But to mourn like Gide because France's old versification system has been destroyed seems to cheapen the problem; as if one wanted to say that the world is shattered because there are no more operas produced like those of Gluck, whom I love especially. (The Anthology, which ends with Mrs. Pozzi and Raymond Radiquet, excludes Claudel and St.-John Perse. Only one passage from the latter concludes the postscript.) The point is not to wonder "s'il est question d'être relu," but to say: I'll write no matter what happens, to keep alive whatever expresses my aliveness.

All these show me the difference between a great man of a great literary continent and a lesser one, who developed in a remote and difficult corner of the earth and is accustomed not to expect any reward—only to throw bottles into the sea.

SUNDAY, SEPTEMBER 4

We went to the Temple of Augustus again to verify and copy the extant syllables from the inscription of Tourmarch Eustathius. This Stathis (ninth to tenth century)—I don't know why I sometimes see him late in his life as a monk—has become in my mind one of the few good friends Ankara has provided me with. One sees the inscription, if one pays attention, on the left as one enters the old monument. It's carved on two cornerstones, one resting on top of the other, each with a broken right side. The second one rests upon the ground. The whole text was restored by Grégoire (information from E. Memboury, Ankara, 2nd edition, 1934). The present fragments I read as follows:

†ΕΠΗϹΤ[ΑΜ]ΕΝΟϹ . . .
ΥΠΕΡΑΡΘΕΝΤΑϹ . . .
ϹΕ ΤΟΝ ΤΟΝ ΟΛΟΝ ΔΙ[ΜΙΟΥΡΓΟΝ]
ΤΟΥΤΟΝ ΜΕ ΡΥϹΕ ΤΟΝ . . .

*George Seferis, "Mythistorema," VII, l. 33.

ΑΝΑΜΑΡΤΗΤΕ ΩϹ . . .
ΘΕϹΜΟΤϹ ΚΑΙ ϹΕΙΡΑϹ ΑΜ[ΑΡΤΙΩΝ]
Η ΓΑΡ ΕΠΙ ΓΗϹ ΑΡΧ[Η]
ΩΠΛΤϹ [ΚΑΙ] ΞΙΦΤϹ ΑΝΔΡ . . .
ϹΟΖΟΜΕΝΟΝ ΜΕ ΠΑ . . .
ΤΕΛΟϹ ΔΕ ΛΤΠΟΝ ΚΑΤ . . .
ΟΛΟϹ ΕΝ ΝΕΚΡΤϹ ΠΡΟϹ . . .
ΤΛΗ ΠΑΡΑΔΟΤΣ ΤΟ ΧΟ[ΙΚΟΝ]
ΡΤϹΙΝ ΤΕ ΕΠΙΓΩΝ ΔΑΚΡ[ΤϹΙ]
ΜΕΤΑ ΟΔΤΡΜΩΝ ΠΑΡ[ΑΚΑΛΩ] *

THURSDAY, SEPTEMBER 8

For four or five days now I have resumed the Cavafy file. I tried to remember again. I read Peridis' book: too much hay to find two needles; a waste of the material at his disposal. I'm not about to examine any details. I'll see what I can do when we return from Constantinople.

SATURDAY, SEPTEMBER 17

These wretched things they are doing—this transformation of Aeschylus into a robot, into a Polyphemus, these flights of rhetoric—are in essence a reflection of themselves. They present a bloated Aeschylus according to their own image and likeness—ugly.

(Helleniki Demiourgia, Sept. 1, 1949)

It would be an interesting study for someone to show that the function of Ate† (in Aeschylus, etc.) is not at root a moral law, but a natural law

---

*Knowing . . . / those exceedingly elevated . . . / Thou the creator of all things / deliver me from these . . . / O sinless One as . . . / laws and bonds of sins / because the command on earth / with weapons and swords man [fully] . . . / rescuing me . . . / but finally . . . / bodily among the dead . . . / matter surrendering the earthly . . . / and hastening deliverance with tears / with lamentations I pray . . . /
†Ate, the goddess of all evil, and daughter of Zeus. In Homer, she is the personification of infatuation or moral blindness. In later times Ate is transformed into an avenger of unrighteousness, like the Furies.

(as, e.g., the law of communicating vessels). See the Pre-Socratics, Anaximander, etc.; see analogues to the Chinese (Meng Tzu, Richards). However, Richards wonders, I think, whether this phenomenon has also functioned in reverse: from the moral to the natural law.

This evening we leave for Constantinople.

MONDAY, SEPTEMBER 19, CONSTANTINOPLE

The house where we landed (the Consulate) is a superannuated Labyrinth. From the south windows you can see the end of the Great Palace and Hagia Sophia. From the north you sometimes see a crazy old woman with bare breasts, howling in foreign languages. They told me she is Armenian. The first resident in this house was a Patriarch of Jersusalem. The result: to reach the bathroom now you must pass through the Patriarch's side-chapel. The cat, a beautiful gray tomcat, is castrated; "fewer problems," they explain.

This afternoon, to the Monastery of Stouditis, after the Castle of the Seven Towers. The light is beautiful. Prisons, the death cell, the wooden pole where they tied the convict to shoot arrows at him; in the middle the narrow, bottomless well, the cesspool where they threw the heads of the beheaded—inexhaustible cruelty.

In the garden of Stouditis in front of the Basilica the smell of the fig tree; a pistachio tree with pistachios(?). The caretaker of the yard, an old man the color of parchment, seated hunched over ready to die, a dried-up fountain.

The walls, a dreadful breakwater; remnant of exhausted strength with nothing to protect anymore. Today's masters have abandoned them to decay; they crumble, yet something still remains.

TUESDAY, SEPTEMBER 27, CONSTANTINOPLE

At the Holy Virgin of Chora—Thomas Whittemore. Here, too, continual destruction. Of the ancient monuments it is the Christian they hate most. Were it not for this persistent old man, even this would have gone the way of the others. Fabrics in the mosaics, their folds; wind in the cypresses of Chora; the mosaic of Mary Taking her First Seven Steps; their "architecture"—what scenery. Young Michael James, grandson of William and grandnephew of Henry James, working as a volunteer cleaning the stones of the mosaics.

Yesterday at Pantelis' taverna. Sanctuary of St. Basil; this amazing phenomenon of survival which is Constantinople; not only of one, but of two Empires; so many men making the gestures of the dead.

FRIDAY, SEPTEMBER 30

Blachernae. Filled with excrement; Kerkoporta.* Walls; cracks; towers standing guard over no one, or cast down like dice. ("The fortune of our own Bishop Constantine Theophylactus conquers.") Gypsy houses; a turkey's cry; the dried trench bed. Eyub—landscape in despair.

OCTOBER, CONSTANTINOPLE

Psamatia. Mouchliotissa Church at Phanar. Turned-off lights; whistle of a ship; the sky "a resurrection."

Buzzing of a fly at daybreak in the bedroom—

"And I, with only a reed in my hands"—(Revelation, 11, 1)

The touch of madness under the big acacias—

Palaces entangled with railroad tracks, like love tokens from other times wrapped in dead locks of hair.

With the vision of a Greece no one understands; and yet it is there, like

*Kerkoporta (Tail Gate), the little gate of the walls of Constantinople, which had been left insecurely bolted; it was through this gate the first Turks entered the city on May 29, 1453.

the olive tree, like the rock, like the homecoming—not made by hands, ineffable; a lodestone.

We are nothing yet, only now are we beginning to discern things that could perhaps come into the light.

FRIDAY, OCTOBER 14, ANKARA

Since noon, Ramazan has been missing; we searched wherever we could; he went off to die. We returned yesterday morning from Constantinople. On Tuesday we put Annoula on the English plane. The nervousness of departure: continual postponements since Monday morning; bad weather in Athens. Thinking about our return to Ankara, we said Ramazan was the only beloved living thing we had in this place. Yesterday we found him in the garden, looking strange; we said that he had forgotten us; he was sick. He wouldn't touch food. He stayed curled up, motionless, amazed. In the afternoon he began to vomit; like that all night. This morning he climbed onto the grape arbor and curled up on the leaves. When I called, he opened his eyes and meowed weakly. When I came home from the office they told me he had disappeared. At dusk we couldn't hold back our tears. This drop of tenderness made us brim over; we were terribly alone.

SUNDAY, OCTOBER 16

Since the day before yesterday I've been arranging papers, countless papers, and grieving for Ramazan. He was my only friend in Ankara, a friend of my own. I can't explain the unexpected, the hyperbolic, the irrational emotional state into which the loss of this small creature has plunged me. It is the circumstance of this little death perhaps; as if he waited for us before dying. Then, I don't know, such a death makes you see the void—that place of his on the grape arbor—from another angle, smaller but clearer, in a more naked way; it is another thing, the ghost of an animal; without resurrection; an absolute loss. The earth seemed horribly inhuman Friday afternoon.

So much dignity in the way he went off to die. He sought the sun constantly, he looked at the fire. A small rough sketch of death; like ships one sees in bottles, with all the details of the original. Death played with him, just as other times he used to play with birds or mice. Motionless, as in the moment of lovemaking, the little household god. No doubt, I put much of myself into this. But what is mine? How strange this is; seriously, how strange.

"And there was no more sea." (Revelations, 21, 1)

"I know thy works that thou art neither cold nor hot." (Revelations, 3, 15)

NOVEMBER

One must be exceptionally great to attain the stature of an old man: Oedipus (at Colonus), Makriyannis—most become rags. This sort seems to get rarer in our times, where men grow old and finish without ever maturing.

Hands in the pockets of a worn-out coat, unshaven,
he came today without knocking at the door . . .

The pomegranates split open by the multitude of stars,
bodies at the uphill climb of night, a galaxy;
we have nothing else
but this embrace,
this breast where inundation diminishes,
where the seed dies—

The hour comes for a stained soul,
without music—

The pigsty was good,
beyond the mud nothing,
like a dream sunk low
in the deep bed;

nothing lower,
and death almost like yours
without premeditation—

"Philoctetes":
Wounded body, wounded land,
Wounded time—

MONDAY, JANUARY 16

Cold. For the first time since our arrival at Ankara all the sparrows, without exception, have disappeared. At night it goes much lower than twenty below.

Since our return from Constantinople: more copying of the diaries; I prepared and sent to Athens the collected edition of poems, 1924–1946; I wrote the letter about the "Thrush." The last two took me several days. On the 12th of the month I took up Cavafy again; if I don't finish him now, I must burn all these manuscripts.

SATURDAY, JANUARY 28

Night of 18–19 January: Angelos.*

*Angelos Seferiadis (1905–1950), Seferis' brother, taught Greek at the U.S. Army Language School in Monterey, California, where he died and is buried.

WEDNESDAY, MARCH 1

The dreadful war nature wages to prevent the Poet from existing.

WEDNESDAY, MARCH 15

Among the books Z was kind enough to send from Paris, I received Stendhal's diary. It begins like this:

"Milan, le 28 Germinal an IX.—J'entreprends d'écrire l'histoire de ma vie jour par jour. Je ne sais si j'aurais la force de remplir ce projet, déjà commencé à Paris. Voilà déjà une faute de français; il y en aura beaucoup par ce que je prends pour principe de ne pas me gêner et de n'effacer jamais." (The emphasis is mine.)

I've been thinking about that passage this week. It's been a long time since I started putting in order my personal notes from 1925 on—sporadically, the year before last; intensively, after our return from Bursa until the end of '49, with the interruption of our autumn trip to Constantinople. I also wrote, much more irregularly, "sans me gêner et sans effacer." But I didn't plan "to write the story of my life, day by day." Day by day we live our life; we don't write it—writing, no matter what you do, is only a part of life.

EVENING

I passed through periods of great doubt concerning the value my works would have. I proceeded in life, all alone, without help (but who has help?), except for two men not connected with letters, and my own perseverance. As I look back on the past, I would call it the perseverance of a Negro. Until 1936 the years were very difficult. Nor do I forget that, after Strophe there were friends who showed me both love and dedication. But I don't mean that; when I say help I mean the man who helps at the critical moments of doubt and accepts, while they're still fresh, your daring attempts. This I lacked.

But now—these days when I am fifty—I know what I am. I know who may accept me and who reject me. I am interested in the former, and, among the latter, in those better than I. I add without hesitation that I pray better ones may appear, even if they efface me from the memory of men. It is not my work that interests me above all else; it is work, without a possessive pronoun, that must live, even if our personal contributions are consumed in it.

I am fully conscious that we do not live in a time when the poet can believe that fame awaits him, but in a time of oblivion. This doesn't make me less dedicated to my beliefs; I am more so. At the same time it causes me to endure with greater peace of mind the indescribable "intellectual" men of Attico-Boeotia.

Thus, just as I published Strophe, just as I published Mythistorema, although others considered my whims crazy, I sat down and undertook, during this stopover at Ankara, the clearing out of these papers—still another "bottle into the sea," personal this time. Who knows, this, too, may help other seafarers like me.

Another reason: to fulfill my release.

SATURDAY, MARCH 25

The Constantinople-Ankara plane crashed, killing our diplomatic courier, a young fellow-employee, John Fleggas.

MONDAY, MARCH 27

With glittering of glass, with silence sang the snow.
This music kills; the sparrows vanished days ago; they went to bury
    their dead.
The stalactites from the trees strike the whining
    cord of a vapid sun.
Let me hear my brother—

Memory, wherever you touch it, hurts.

"Heart encircled by a snake."

"There is no old age for this miasma" (<u>Seven</u> <u>Against</u> <u>Thebes</u>, I. 682)

APRIL 5, HOLY WEDNESDAY

Last Sunday (Palm Sunday): To Konya. We left at 8:30, and were back on Monday at 16:30: approximately 270 kilometers, four and a half hours by car. The road (the new one) straight, crosses the Salt Desert, the most monotonous I've ever seen. Harsh gray in color, and all around, as soon as you leave the suburbs of Ankara behind, absolutely nothing. Very few villages, mud houses. The motherland of Karamanitis.

At Konya, waking up about three in the morning, outside a full moon: "Horreur, tout est donc sous un éteignoir!" Then passionately: "Through death he has conquered death."

We stayed at the Seljuk Hotel. The idea of "éteignoir" suggested in my sleep, I imagine, by the dark blue dome of the tekke of the Mevlevi [Whirling Dervishes] and the deadness of the people who live all around it today.

The graceful carpets in the tekke are the most beautiful we've ever seen. Everywhere in the city lawyers' shingles. A small museum; many Greco-Roman gravestones and two or three sarcophagi; many lions in three-dimension sculpture or bas-relief; the museum director says the lion is the guardian of the dead (?).

The Seljuk monuments, pure Persian or Arabic art. At Karatay, a mosque and Indje minaret, the dome open to the sky and, underneath, a square cistern, dried up now, where once they studied in the water the mirrored movement of the stars; one thinks of nights with faces leaning over, transfixed there.

At the market, a small courtyard, with shops around this patio. When they see a foreigner they ask extravagant prices for junk. They were selling a brass baking pan, with its inscription awkwardly engraved between two crosses, "Sophia 1809." On the way back, at Çihanbeyli, where we stopped, a marble stele leaning against the railing of the small square with the inscription:

ΛΕΩΝΙΔΗC
ΠΛΑΝΤΑC
ΔΙΔΩΤΗΡ*

Konya makes you recall the phrase one heard in my childhood: "He's from the depths of Anatolia." At the pastry shop, where we had break-fast, a different expression on the proprietor's face; but he's a refugee from Serres. When he came, he tells us, before the Balkan wars, people here knew nothing about making pastry. There are two other pastry-makers in Konya, also from Serres. I've been thinking about this minor Greek civilization, not that of the intellectual currents but the one that permeates everyday behavior—the sweets, the cultivation of the earth, the art of the builder, the insignificant gestures. Konya consoles you for living in Ankara; it could be worse.

GOOD FRIDAY, APRIL 7

An Epitaphios at the office which had been turned into a chapel. Touching, in spite of faltering voices and such. Suggestion of sounds and words. The rite of our church is surely related to ancient tragedy.

WEDNESDAY, APRIL 12

Last January the subject of Cavafy ended irrevocably—for me. Today I bid it goodbye. After '46 it gave a few glimmers, then plunged to the bottom. I had sorted out all the papers from Poros and later that might jog my memory on one topic or another; the others went into the wastebasket. I felt relief. Sometimes our life, with its imperceptible development, progresses faster than our works. And perhaps most

*Leonides / Plantas / Donor

difficult in my work is that we don't know how long we must persist
or when we must abandon certain works which have started to become
hindrances. Well, Cavafy, in times of stress, is not strong enough to help.
If I were asked whom I would call "strong" in the sense I have in mind,
I would instinctively name Makriyannis.

POROS, ATHENS. 1946–47

Although Cavafy is often gnomic, he is not a man to throw all his authority
behind a general moral conclusion. In conversations with Lechonitis, what
he stresses most is "particularity": "the poet of course does not confront
generalities"; or: "the poem is particular"; or even "Cavafy's poems . . .
were not written as representative of a general condition of humanity—
but as particulars (partiels)." Cavafy's spoken apothegms should be read
with great caution—always taking into account the guidelines provided
for us by his poems. These contain the fundamental meaning and are
the only expressions of his that cannot hide behind artifice. Cavafy's
conversations can easily lead one astray; they have led many astray
already. When one is asked what Cavafy means by his use of the word
"particularity," one sees mainly that Cavafy wants to defend himself
against those who have accused him of pessimism (L 43).* We know
how sensitive he was, how quick to react to the slightest criticism.

On the subject of pessimism I would say: Cavafy has before him a reality
which he sees and expresses in the most succinct manner. This reality
(of memory, of old age, of lost pleasure, of deceit), whether raw, dry, or
whatever, cannot be called pessimistic. If, perforce, I had to characterize
it, I certainly could not call it beautiful. What follows concerns each
man's personal opinion, not just about poetry but about the future
of humanity.

Cavafy says further: "I do not like analyses within the short story or
the novel. I prefer a dry, unadorned description of events, without
comments. That is why I like description of manners so much. I can reach
my own conclusion that way."† Here too, as above, when he speaks about

*George Lechonitis, Kavafika autoscholia (Alexandria, 1942).
† Yangos Pieridis, Kavafis (Athens, Orion, 1943).—G. S.

particularity, Cavafy has, I believe, one thing in his mind: <u>objectivity</u>. With this objectivity, Cavafy describes character or, if we insist, the acting out of his world. Cavafy is not a man of great moral pronouncements, as I have said. He is not likely to rumble, like the Thunder of <u>The Waste Land</u>, "Give, sympathize, control;" but the givens of the problem— the dryness of the sources of emotion, the desire for rebirth—he feels in his own body, anthropomorphically; he's a Greek and he doesn't have a long tradition of moralistic preaching behind him. (However, because Makriyannis was a Greek he can write letters to God or conclude agreements with St. John.) Cavafy does not give advice; he gives himself to his work, and through this he portrays his world. In this way he expresses a fundamental problem of our life with great clarity. He doesn't broadcast his convictions; he expresses the conduct of certain elements in our life. From that point on, it's up to us to judge and draw conclusions.

The "Barbarians": petrified "inaction" and a whisper. See on the contrary, the agility of the Lares. Cold humor: not "wit" (esprit). The element of wit is light, dances, somersaults. Humor rambles, serious, indifferent. Sometimes it staggers or stumbles, but it is never "sparkling." It is a serious distortion of our life (see Edward Lear). Cavafy's humor is sometimes so serious that you can't distinguish it from himself. His existence is humor, an existence at once tragic and humorous in a hollow world that doesn't know where it is going (no, tragically ironic). That's why he was so often caricatured in both writing and life. There are so many composites in him that one transforms another. Perhaps it is this I seek to express when I use the Homeric Proteus so frequently.

Diaeos, Kritolaos, Archaeos, Lathyros, Demetrius Soter, Venizelos, Constantine—the eternal Greek history. How else can one write about politics, that is, if he wants to touch more deeply the human essence and not be reduced to political wrangling? How many Demetrioi (Soteres) were there in our everyday political life of the interwar years; when we used to talk about the alliance of Herakleides and Balas!

In the Middle East we lived the political and apothegmatic Cavafy to the utmost. When we transported this manner of thinking to Greek soil Cavafian common sense spread to the rhetoric of the newspapers; a few days ago, Eleftheria (December 4, 1946): on national demands, "not with the coward's entreaties and complaints"; and, before that, also in Eleftheria: "he became homeless and poor"; or last May in Vima: "The destiny of this blue miracle to guard Thermopylae even though it knows that Ephialtes will appear in the end and the Medes will pass," etc., etc. Thus, Cavafy appears to be the most frequently cited Greek poet in the daily newspapers—not in the arts columns on the second page, but in the political editorials. At the beginning of the war Sikelianos called one of his own poems, "Haute Actualité." Cavafy becomes basse actualité. The only difference is that in Sikelianos' case the emphasis falls upon haute and in Cavafy's upon actualité. Does this indicate that the "market" responds better to Cavafy than to the ivory-tower despots?

Cavafy (who had nothing to do with the troubles in '97, '09, '12, etc.) appears to grow (politically and socially) outside of Greece. He encounters the Helladic destiny, I believe, after the Asia Minor catastrophe. I suppose that is why, during his first period, he is judged superficially. People began to take him more seriously only around the thirties, when that drama became conscious, the historic and contemporary drama of the race.

With the outcry of those whose main concern is to frustrate the man of the opposing faction (154) Cavafy left us.* He departed from our world at a time when the last act of our drama had ended: catastrophe was upon us. He was an exhausted, bent old man, mumbling about images he used to see in Alexandria. Very few listened to him, and fewer understood his unintelligible muttering. What else but muttering, amid the massive hubbub of autarchical Europe, could the broadsides which he printed at Kasimatis' and Ionas' printing shop be? It is not surprising that no one heard him. Great men vanished amidst those vociferations. He was a messenger, however. Had Hitler listened to him, what the Chancel-

*"On the Outskirts of Antioch" (154). See Poems by C. P. Cavafy, translated by John Mavrogordato, with an introduction by Rex Warner (London, 1971), pp. 198–199. Consequent references will be to this edition which corresponds to the Greek: C. P. Cavafy, Poiemata, 2nd ed. (Athens, 1948). Numbers in parentheses refer to poem numbers.

lery of Berlin saw in the last days of April 1945 would not have taken place. But what Caesar reads the writings of Artemidorus the Grammarian? What man like that will listen if you say: heed Aeschylus, the deed you want to do will destroy many worthy things as well as you yourself. Even Aeschylus in our present plight is a kind of ineffectual Artemidorus: "Thus runs the world away."

Cavafy's last fifteen years are not only a period of crisis in Europe but even more so of Hellenism. They are the years when this phenomenon appears for the first time in our entire history: the polarization on Greek soil of the whole Hellenic nation, of the Hellenic diaspora as they would say now. A phenomenon which we have not yet become aware of.

Deinokratis' book is written with complete Egyptian mistrust, and sometimes with meanness.

Julian presents a problem for Cavafy, he is a splinter on the horizon, one who unsettles him because he wanted to change fate, to operate outside of the world order. He is worse than a problem; he is a sort of illegal competition. And, like Julian, Cavafy longs for the return of the ancients, of their pleasure: "For him the gods have not died at all," or: "he will bring back the worship of our gods" ("If Dead Indeed" 91). But not like that puritan who is dedicated to an ideological cause, the one who is not "partly . . . partly"; not like that rustic, "most ridiculous" in our large Greek cities, that hypocrite, braggart, childish and prudish one. Apollonius is another matter; he nourishes the mud and is our contemporary, like Madame Blavatsky (see Henry Miller).

Cavafy of course, belongs to the other tradition, that of katharevousa.* Regardless of whether we all are to some extent scholarly, I want to limit the topic. Notice that, in his hands, as he proceeds, his pedantic

*Katharevousa (Purist language), is a form of Modern Greek which was artificially created shortly before the Greek Revolution of 1821 and further developed during the nineteenth century. It is based on the forms of ancient Greek grammar with a somewhat simplified syntax, and contains many neologisms. Although it was never spoken by the Greek people, this is the official language of the Greek state.

language loses its fat little by little, shrinks, and may sometimes become shriveled, in order to seek and unite with the parallel oral tradition, the demotic. On the other hand the demotic needed some kind of refining agent; it found Cavafy.

Nanis wrote me (he had told me this once before) that Cavafy listened carefully to any conversation that caught his ear in the street, at the stock exchange; in fact he sought out such occasions; he even admitted that he was an eavesdropper. In the sense of the eavesdropper, I think he builds, on an Anglo-Constantinopolitan substratum, his own demotic language.

His own demotic—one can define this language if one is able to discern the distance separating the language of Cavafy's maturity from the katharevousa of his repudiated poems—which is continually diminishing and, after "Before the Statue of Endymion," disappears entirely, as well as the distance separating it from Karyotakis' mixed journalistic language.* Cavafy wrote in his own language, but those who attempted to imitate him wrote in the language of no one at all.

The small amount of published work left by Cavafy is a rhapsody, a stage position with all the aspects of barrenness, i.e., as the dictionary defines the word: "the inability of a man or woman to impregnate or be fertilized, non-bearing, sterility." "Barren love," Cavafy says. Skimming through The Waste Land we see clearly this barrenness. There, too, the handsome young man is dead (Phlebas and those who play the role of "the dead God"—the graves and shrouds begin earlier in Cavafy), just as the woman is barren (the chess game, etc.). I would say in particular that in this epic, which both the Greek and the Anglo-Latin write in astonishingly similar frameworks (historical sentiment, learning, old age, cruel sarcasm), the difference between them, contrary to what has been said about Cavafy, is that the Puritan is more scrupulous in his creation than the Greek Orthodox. For the progress of consciousness in Eliot (choice of teachers, etc.) see his works of criticism; as for Cavafy's critical ability, with the exception of a few sparks, it seems to me of no consequence. I do not

*"Before the Statue of Endymion" (59), p. 78.

mean of course that which is apparent in his verses, which is another matter, but the few critical texts he has left. No matter how much Cavafy is called introspective, a dissembler (I'm thinking of Diderot), calculating, etc., the question is one of characteristics, which I have no difficulty accepting if they persist; in my opinion, however, the characteristics are those of Cavafy the ordinary man, not of the <u>poet</u>. Almost from the start Cavafy seems constrained, by the logic of his sensibility and by tradition, to a myth, the myth of the dead god, that passion of the submersion of a world (regardless, that is, of whether or not he retains in his conversations various eccentricities or Wildeian rages). And this passion, this staging of the emotional complexes of our world, I would see, no matter how strange it might seem, not as a hothouse flower, carefully cultivated, but as a wild herb that has sprouted at a corner of the road of Hellenic tradition. The work of the Greek has a development which, if not natural, is nevertheless <u>in accordance with nature</u>. Eliot's accordance with nature we'll find elsewhere.

Up to a fairly advanced age (maturity), Cavafy seems to remain at a very low level; he seems unable to rise above a certain very mediocre "ceiling" (as it is called in aviation: ceiling, plafond). What happens at and beyond a certain point? How does he cross that threshold? Here's a question that interests me—not only about Cavafy but in general.

I once heard one younger poet saying to another, in a critical tone: "You of course write beautifully" (see "<u>Days</u> <u>M.E.</u>").* Not in the sense we say that so-and-so writes with many flourishes, without content, with many embellishments, but as we say to someone we envy for the material comfort fortune has endowed him with: "You of course clip coupons." The other in vain tried to explain that he had sweated to learn the Greek language he was writing. I was irked by the invidious tone of the first; now I think sympathetically about that embittered man. For one who crosses the threshold, how many have remained below the ceiling? How many pitchers are broken for each that survives?

The example of Cavafy is one of the most striking. Up to a certain point

*Days, Middle East, is a part of Seferis' unpublished diary.

he appears to be hanging by a cotton thread; you think the slightest touch could cast him into forgotten ruins. What miracle allowed him to cross the threshold? I say it is faith in himself, the difficult acceptance of his own sincerity: imprecise, meaningless phrases, perhaps. I would like to know more.

As for those who emphasize Cavafy's erotic perversions, the same happened with Baudelaire at the beginning; he was the idol of the perverse—Black Aphrodite, sapphism, sadism, impotency. In the end, all these were no longer an issue. Who looks at Baudelaire in that way any more? Here's a topic for an essay: a comparison (an incalculably disproportionate comparison) of the criticism of Cavafy and the criticism of Baudelaire.

My fancy sometimes reaches even this absurd limit: if all the poets of the world were permitted to use one word only—the same word—the good poets would still find a way to differ from each other and create with this single word different personal poems (a thought that verges on Zen).

"Le merveilleux nous enveloppe et nous abreuve comme l'atmosphère; mais nous ne le voyons pas" (Baudelaire, Pléiade, II, 135). "Il m'arrivera souvent d'apprécier un tableau uniquement par la somme d'idées ou de rêveries qu'il apportera dans mon esprit" (ibid., 147). "L'être pensant qui n'a que soi pour but souffre d'une vacance abominable" (where?).

The void in Cavafy, exactly this abominable vacance (pleasure, art). If Cavafy had had more readily available means, he would have become physiologically, as I said, an inglorious descendant of the katharevousa writers, or he would have perished in the void of a man with no interest apart from himself. I think his difficulties, which made him totally unsuited to rhetoric, saved him. With regard to this, his example is unique in a land marked by the curse of the empty word. He was saved, I think, by exactly the thing they accuse him of: his bareness. It is strange to speak so about a man who emerges from such a rhetorical tradition.

As the years pass Cavafy does not see images, he sees motions, lines of motion. He uses no metaphors, but his entire work is a metaphor. That is why there are so many verbs. The "Old Man" is perhaps still an image;

the last poem about Julian (154) a pandemonium of motions. Cavafy originally wanted to be a painter, but the lack of motion in works of painting made him change his mind. And yet something perhaps is left from this old inclination, a choreography, I would say. The child's answer Roger Fry mentions may illuminate my thought: when asked how he drew, the little one answered: "First I think, and then I draw a line round my think."

This untalented man, Cavafy, makes poetry nonetheless. He's the reverse of Solomos, who has great talent and can't progress. A comparison would be worthwhile. Both write in a language they are continually learning.

"His Christianity was also a 'logical' consequence, a kind of compromise he had accepted . . . I remember that he was indifferent to the 'sacrament' . . . but he didn't like others to speak to him against our religion because he found this undecorous for us Greeks" (Nanis' letter).

But even if we look at the poems of Cavafy that deal with Christianity, we see that religion interests him, I would say, either from the aspect of criticizing the characters, revealing men who do not bother to restrain their desires or who find refuge in it in "critical moments" (30), like Manuel Comnenus (55) or Ignatius (68), or from the aspect of "partly . . . partly . . . ," a phenomenon of life which always attracts him. Beyond this he seems a nonparticipant in matters of religion, and sometimes quite far removed. For instance, in one of the first poems considered Christian, he writes "There when I enter the church of the Greeks." One wonders what the poet's religion is. I don't think an Orthodox would say "when I enter the church of the Orthodox." Cavafy speaks at least like a man "partly pagan, and partly Christian" (50), or like a man of another faith. It would be naive, it seems to me, to conclude from the priest's son at the Serapion (128), unique in his belief, that Cavafy was among the truly faithful. This young man shows only the fanaticism of a neophyte. As for Myres (143), that's another story, and can lead to opposite conclusions; let's leave it for another time.*

*"What Things Are Dangerous" (30), p. 45; "Manuel Comnenus" (55), p. 73; "The Tomb of Ignatius" (68), p. 87; "Myres: Alexandria: A.D. 340" (143), p. 179.

In the foreword of "C.-T.S.E." (o altra cosa), if they are published in a separate booklet:

Maybe this is not the Cavafy you've been accustomed to; maybe I have emphasized points that startled you: I tried, you'll say, to relate two terribly dissimilar physiognomies. Maybe. However, among the many ways that there are to study poets, the simplest, it seems to me, is the best: to look at what their works show us. And it is not improbable that they show things which we were looking for; "which we would not have sought if we had not found them already," as someone else says; or, to remember the ancient sage, "knowledge is memory." Thus, poets complement us and we complement them. I do not intend to advise arbitrariness when we read poems. A poem is not reason enough for us to unleash our imagination in reckless wanderings. Rather, what I want to say is this: that poets, if their poetry is good, draw on a deep-rooted experience of life, which all of us, young and old, have within ourselves; how much we feel this, I don't know. These are the roots through which they communicate with us. What forms, what vestments this common experience, this common feeling of life, will take in a historical moment no one can tell. It depends, I think, not only upon the idiosyncrasy of the individual who expresses himself but also upon many intellectual, social, and political mores of the time. A poem written from a purely erotic impulse may become in another era the expression of the feeling of human humiliation, of deceit, of degradation, because the era in some way has brought such sentiments to the surface; it has made them, let's say, public. And the praise of a rose or a ray of sunlight may convey the impression of human grandeur at moments when human grandeur flashes like lightning, as Solomos would say. These variations, as time passes, indicate that poems are alive and are nourished; they have the power to complement us and they ask us to complement them. If poetry were not sustained by this kind of human solidarity, in this human community, it wouldn't have lived very long. Poetry does not express truths in the scientific meaning of the word, nor does it discover philosophies and life theories; it uses science and the philosophy of others, if it needs them. Poetry is not for personal confessions; if it makes them, it is not they that save it. It does not try to express the personality of the poets, but, as Eliot has written, tries rather to abolish it. But in doing this, it expresses another personality that belongs to everyone; whosoever loses his life will find it, the Gospel says. Thus, let us not ask from the poet, in order to understand him, the petty, everyday details of his life which we think he is expressing. These petty events, if they have become poetry, are events belonging to you and me, and to those who have gone before, and to those who will come after us. If it were not so, poetry would not exist. You can make the experiment yourselves. Read a rhapsody of Homer and see if whether, at the parts that move you, what you feel is merely an archaeological reference alone, or if perhaps it is a sentiment nurtured by all the human experience that has occurred from that ancient era down to your present moment.

. . . In the era of the first Cavafyism, the Alexandrian was, for the critics, an imposter or a maniacal old man who was playing the game of a maddened ostrich; for his admirers, who hurt him even more, a salacious whisperer of ambiguous eroticisms and the rest. We saw him with different eyes, when we saw the world, too, with different eyes. When the younger generation emerged from the experience of the first great war—which was for us an experience much more horrendous than for other nations—they had, at least in the early interwar years, the delusion of triumph; for us that war was ending in an unprecedented catastrophe. A catastrophe which Europe did not notice at that time; Europe had to arrive at the events of 1938 in order fully to comprehend its meaning, for it looked strikingly similar to other contemporary collapses. Nevertheless, the harvest of victory was for us, from the outset, a harvest of ruins . . .

. . . I hope for an understanding, with the necessary nuances, which wouldn't overlook the principle that in art nothing can be expressed inflexibly unless it concerns very bad art. That from the moment we accept a work as living, we must simultaneously decide that it, too, has its own unforeseen destiny. That our designations, our analyses, our interpretations, our aphorisms may well be wonderful things but are at the same time dangerous—even if they derive from the poet himself. Before writing about a poetic work, the honest critic always keeps in mind a silent agreement with the honest reader that his writings are only attempts to approach and can in no way substitute for the poem; that they must be forgotten quickly so that we may return to the poem. I am compelled to state again and again these self-evident things, because everyday experience shows me that to a great degree we address ourselves to a public that seeks crutches; living bodies frighten it because they are strange, or so it thinks. But how else could it be? Life is strange. And, if we don't see this, we must either say nothing or resort to that beclouded rhetoric that knows how to lull everything to sleep . . .

. . . My job is not the job of a philologist—not that I scorn philology. My job is to drop hints, if it's worth the trouble, and if they can endure.

In "Cavafy-Eliot" I behave less like a critic, who comments, if I may say so, on the dialogue of the two poets, than like an eavesdropper. My own view I should express in another long essay, apart from these two. Perhaps such an opportunity will occur. However, I must confess that this third-person position amused me.

I am thinking about the feeling of history Eliot speaks of. I felt it formed within me five or six years before I even heard of its existence. Eliot helped me perceive with greater clarity a feeling I had tried to express at that time—not through criticism but in the form of the novel, and of course I failed; I'm not a novelist. In those years (1926) I was reading Gide, Villon, and Rabelais, and I was discovering Makriyannis with enthusiasm.

. . . Eliot is the mathematical type in foreign literature who comes nearest (mutatis mutandis) to the mathematical type of Cavafy. I like to relate men to each other. Some think it is more important to express even their dialogue in the form of a monologue; it's the mania of originality. I would turn even my monologue into dialogue, if I could.

. . . I always have the impression that each phrase I write is my last.

ANKARA. OCTOBER 1949-END OF JANUARY 1950
I find the psalmody quite amusing:

Let us pray for the most pious Jovian.

How curious Neo-Hellas is. Byzantium, on one side, in the hands of a character named Cavafy, on the other, in the hands of a priest's son from Skiathos, Papadiamantis, a humble man* (also with repressed sensuality). It would be worth the trouble for someone to write a separate book, where he would analyze how Byzantine, as they say, and how Neohellene Papadiamantis is. It's one thing, I think, to be a Byzantine (because you thought you were), and another to derive (from yourself) elements that have survived with you (with the tradition). In essence, the problem I would be concerned with is whether Papadiamantis represents another aspect of the Neohellenic phenomenon of which one exponent is Makriyannis.

How Cavafy's family and milieu see the Greeks (not a rare phenomenon anyway, among the populations of the Nation): "But the Greeks, my dear Kostakis, have made a mess. Now they let the Powers do to them whatever they wish" (letter from his mother, May 14, 1897; M.P. 86).† Or his friend Rallis: "My cousin introduced me to a distant relative of ours, a certain Negrepontis of about my age, . . . a totally corrupted Greek, as Papazis would call him, . . . but who is, in my opinion, the most charming character in the world. He grew up in England and hardly knows one word of Greek and despises immensely anything concerning Greece" (his letter from Athens, June 17, 1882; M.P. 28, translation from the English of M.P.).

For a long time now I've been thinking that perhaps it was Pallis' translation of the Iliad that gave Cavafy the idea of occupying himself with Homeric themes. Now I read in M.P. 74 that Pallis' marked translation was found in his library.

And this (noted in Nirvanas' Asophos, M.P. 75) that shows so clearly his desire for a bare objectivity: "As few descriptions as possible. Describe

*Alexandros Papadiamantis (1851–1911), novelist and short story writer.
†Michalis Peridis, I Zoe Kai To Ergo Tou K. P. Kavafi [The Life and Work of C. P. Cavafy], (Ikaros, 1948).—G. S.

only what you have seen, yourself alone, and what you are sure you have seen."

Lamia (1893). Prose often terrible; it reminds me of the language of old translations of The Three Musketeers: "Fixedly gazing steadfastly at her" and so on and so on. Lines (of the translation) such as "The Tarantines entertain themselves," "Horace in Athens," etc. Often a stride that does not exist in Keats; his line of verse cramps him, overflows. Were such exercises the starting point for the strides he used so much later? Dreadful what a worthy poet can start from! I'm thinking of when he remarks on Keats' Lamia: "It is written with the ease characteristic of the quill of the true (emphasis mine) poet."

His logic in the study of Keats. The attraction which luxury, decorum, exerts upon him. His eroticism: "Illness of decay" (for Lycius), "Every superb pleasure is paid for," and this, worth noting: "of whom the Greek myth related the bloodthirsty eros, who transforms death into carnal pleasure" (again my emphasis).

The amazing change that takes place when Cavafy enters the phase of his distilled poems keeps returning to my mind. We have not studied this phase enough; what it shows us about his devotion to his old idols; and, if it remained stable, what made it suddenly change form.

In the final analysis, memory has one horizon—whether the days of 200 B.C. or of A.D. 340 or 1911. The sense of memory is not fragmented, regardless of whether there are gaps, lacunae. Fundamentally, there is no disruption of the continuity. We separate it into compartments because our thoughts are paratactical and we place them paratactically. When we see Cavafy noting, "We know it, we are time" (M.P. 82), Bergson or not, we see clearly how the sense of memory functions in him (see also Proust, Retrouvé, 253). The question is not one of retrospection as one reads in the chapter of a history book, or various "intellectual" conveyances, as some would say. It is a question of an emotional agent that I do not know if we are at this moment trained enough to discern.

Note. "Precisely the first characteristic of the artist is overlooked: peace of soul and great surrender in the face of things which stir indignation and the rebukes of common men" (M.P. 82, emphasis mine).

English. With the exception of legends about his linguistic molding in childhood, which may not have been clearly verified (Cavafy must have been subjected to many English influences—family, mother, travel), Xenopoulos notes that he had a "slightly English accent." He is completely bilingual and M.P. informs us that he used English in correspondence, his commentary on texts, his notes (63), in headings of personal files (84).

"The brave men of pleasure" bothered me from the start.* And the admirers of this bravery bothered me even more. I remember a summer evening in Athens before the war. A friend recited with a terribly vibrant voice: "hair as if from Greek statues taken."† He succeeded in nothing more than giving me the impression that he was quoting a poet talking about wigs. And now that so much has passed and so much has happened, when I think about it seriously, it seems to me that these "brave men" have left a bad wrinkle on the Alexandrian.

THURSDAY, APRIL 20

The AFP from Detroit: "La guerre des nerfs risque, lors d'un prochain conflit, à devenir une réalité concrète: les services chimiques de l'armée américaine mettront au point un gaz qui affecterait directement le système nerveux de la population et de l'armée d'un futur enemi. Cette révélation fut faite hier soir par le général McAuliffe, au service de la Société Américaine de Chimie" (Press Agency of the East).‡ Why not? These are times of stupidity; stupifying weapons in the place of lethal ones, for victory in war, for law and order in peace.

*"I Went" (40), p. 57.
†"So Much I Gazed" (69), p. 88.
‡The war of nerves risks, in the event of an imminent conflict, becoming a concrete reality: the chemical services of the American Army will put into effect a gas which will directly affect the nerous system of the population and the army of a future enemy. This revelation was made last night by General McAuliffe in the service of the American Chemical Society.

SATURDAY, APRIL 22

The Helleniki (?) Demiourgia (??) again: Jan. 15, '50. Now it has put Sophocles on the spot. It begins: "Aeschylus leaves the Thymele dragging behind himself the frenzied clatter of Corybants—an enormous and dreadful troupe of demigods and monsters" (sic). Aeschylus "utters oracles with a mouth wreathed in epileptic froth . . . ," whereas Sophocles "did not like the megatheres, the inflexible dinosaurs and mammoths of Aeschylus' tragic dramaturgy" (sic and sic again).

When our Academicians proclaim their proper Greek tradition with such bullies' tricks, what will their poor little pupils do?

WEDNESDAY, MAY 3

"It is possible for this very globe to be disintegrated" (sic). When an ordinary clerk writes like this what's left for Saint John the Divine (of Revelations)?

At night, 21:00. M. left for Constantinople-Athens. The train started out like an armada, amidst a rainstorm with thunderbolts. I went by the Androklidises', then home; I tried to orient myself in the new loneliness. Pleasant that everything is tidy and orderly, but a pile of habits protest, as if you were driving a new car for the first time.

THURSDAY, MAY 4

In the morning again to the Station for Oromedon. There was Fratti too, superbusy waiting for Telesilla. She stepped down from the train adorned, shining, like a bonbon. News from Athens; they tell me of such machinations that if one had transcribed them from the ethical to the material world he would have devised a superb play for Grand Guignol. But now these things are bread and butter; in other times they would have impressed me and I would have noted them, fancy that.

Waiting for the train, I was thinking that the life of every community of men seems to revolve around something: a park, the marketplace, the post office, the central square, or the brothel. Here it revolves around the railroad station. You would think that the entire population of the city might embark someday on the train, unknowingly, without regret, emptying it from end to end. It was destined that Ankara be for me too, for almost three years now, a way station.

At noon I ate at the Oromedons'. The occasion ended in complete boredom, so I came home early and lay down reading the <u>Arabian Nights</u> "Story of Aziz and Aziza." I slept for about an hour. Then I warmed some coffee and took a tranquilizer. Before I sat down at my desk I heard the nightingale straining its throat madly. I begin to get used to the quiet house; I feel more comfortable than last night.

SUNDAY, MAY 7

The bad thing is not that we are influenced by foreign ideas in Greece (how could it be otherwise?), the bad thing is that we are never prepared for fresh ideas; we prefer them seasoned or kept frozen until they become articles for mass export. That's what's unfortunate: the thoughtless distortion of this dead heap.

TUESDAY, MAY 9

The rain doesn't stop; you feel its chill stinging. Always totally alone in Ankara; all around me the social rabble that certainly "eats away" metal like a chemical liquid. Where does it eat?

The house has again dressed itself in green leaves. The garden trees touching my window reveal much of Aphrodite! The attraction of an unknown body; these withered fleshes that surround me are (for me) the most terrible outrage that could happen these days.

Yesterday. In the afternoon, poetry for about an hour. Limbs unbearably unexercised; I've known it, but I felt it again, terrified.

In the evening at "Souregia"; the Minister of Magog's dinner. As I chatter
the usual nonsense with the wife of one of his secretaries, I notice that
it is a great indiscretion to ask these people where they were born. She
herself, a plump harem girl, was born and raised in Algiers. "And your
husband?" I asked. She hesitated to answer: "I think, in Egypt," she said
finally. He stared at us grim and speechless. Newcomers to their homeland,
newcomers to their language; a very interesting experiment, as they say.
I would like to have known their deeper psychological reactions, not the
surface ones. But they do not confide easily; they are well armored
with their obstinate fanaticism—not without heroism, I must add.

THURSDAY, MAY 10

Why didn't you say that you would come
that I might spread before my bed
my heart's blood for a carpet
and from my eyes black velvet,
night traveler?

Why didn't you say that you would come
that I might spread for you my body,
the silken flesh of youth,
and the dew of my face
so you might lie and sleep with me?

(Arabian Nights, Mardrus)

WEDNESDAY, JUNE 21

Let the houses become habitations of the dead;
you will find different lands, other cities,
but you will find no other soul like your own.

(Arabian Nights, Mardrus)

THURSDAY, JUNE 22

We set out from Ankara in E.'s jeep, at 6:15. His chauffeur's name is
Yusuf; he's a Circassian; his French always ends with the words et cetera.
Beautiful summer; even Anatolia's wilderness has lost its grimness:
"Still life," but this time successful: yellow tones; dark blue in the fields;
dark blue birds flutter every so often near us. I was told they are "Anatolian
magpies."

Sivrihisar at about 11:00. Coffee; some humanity in the architecture of
the houses; whatever it is, it comforts. The old wooden mosque (Ulu
Djami); its pillars a forest, like masts in a narrow harbor.

Lunch at Eskisehir. We wandered through the streets and shops dealing
in old coins (E. hunts them passionately). Shops where they work "foam
of the sea" (a noteworthy handicraft of the place); they carve this stone
wet, then it becomes soft like soap. But the significant spectacle for me
is the carriages. You'd think all the luxurious wheeled vehicles of another
day in Europe and Central Europe—landaus, victorias, coupés—had
ended up here; under the dust you discern signs of former luster: expensive
wrinkled leathers, choice velvets in the disemboweled seats; and this shut-
in appearance, haunted, you could say, by that luxury. I got the impression that I had met a notorious Parisian woman, staggering, toothless,
and aged, in a brothel of this sad district.

We wanted to head toward Kütahya, but took the wrong road. The jeep
is not a comfortable beast of burden; whether the road is good or bad
it pulls apart your spine. E. insists on keeping the canvas top down so the
air can circulate—but only the dust circulates. Vain effort to convince
him to the contrary. He realized it himself later, after we had turned
completely white up to our eyebrows, like snowmen.

19:15 at Kütahya (385 km.). The hotel looked impressive; I asked for
bath, stupid; I had forgotten Konya. Hotels in Turkish provinces (I don't
mean of course centers like Bursa or Constantinople, etc.) are all alike;
even when they are built pretentiously, they end up as inns. No water in

the room; you wash next to the toilet; but there's always a pair of slippers or clogs—the hotel provides them—in front of the bed. Winter or summer they give you for cover a quilt with the sheet sewn onto it. A clean sheet usually, but who can be sure they change it for each traveler? The streets of Kütahya are full of shops; they sell pottery of this name; now a terribly debased art, as generally happens with tourist handicrafts.

We strolled around a little, ate badly, and slept marvelously.

We came outside of the walls. Who frightened us?
No one was out there; dark blue colors on the ground; dark blue birds.
Sometimes huge rocks, glittering like mirrors,
and the herald with golden heels
dressed his nakedness with a blue fluttering of wings—

FRIDAY, JUNE 23

Departure from Kütahya at 6:30. The mountains are beginning to become more human. About twenty kilometers before Gediz we stopped at a mountain spring. A young shepherd, under eighteen, all in patches, graceful, was playing his flute. We called him over, and I gave him half a pound; he had never seen so large a coin. He explained that he couldn't go to school because he must tend the flock. His knapsack was buckled with an oak clasp carved by his father; he gave it to me for another half pound. Gediz is nothing, but it was market day; the most impressive figure there was a vigorous white billygoat with a very black collar.

Uşak at 11:30, 136 km. from Kütahya. We ate here at noon. The shade from the trees has a different feeling; you already sense you aren't far from the seashore. We always hunt for coins for E. Very bad road from little past Usak up to where the trails to Denizli begin; we traveled in a sea of dust. I took the wheel of the jeep. Somewhere near there we met the orange Road Service truck; it had come as an honor escort for E. who had notified the authorities beforehand. Fortunately I am an unofficial companion. I stayed in the jeep; we drove ahead much faster and waited

for them for some time at Baba Dag before we took the road down.
On the surrounding mountainpeaks a livelier substance, different color;
Ionia begins. Each time I leave the Ankara steppe a huge load is lifted from
me. At Denizli (336 km.) we had just about two hours of daylight. We
found a shower and lukewarm water, a great gift.

Another country engineer was waiting for us, together with a Greek-
speaking officer, one of those resettled from Lemnos. The police use a lot
those who know Greek—Cretans or others. We went around to various
outdoor restaurants, looking for food. They all had covered platforms—for
the bands, I suppose. Now they seem to be used as warehouses for chairs
or other broken things.

Freshness of vegetation at Denizli; fevers may exist there, but I am
enjoying this freshness. The women around here almost without exception wear red dresses. It's beautiful to see them walking along, with the
wide, wavy folds, without that muffled appearance you see elsewhere.
Late, before lying down (the nearby open-air movie house was bothering
me with the mechanical bombast of some terrible passion), I went to the
window and saw such a group pausing; then this chorus walked on,
vanishing into the night of the unknown city.

SATURDAY, JUNE 24

In the morning (7:00) from Denizli to Hierapolis. On the way, Laodicea:
"you are neither cold nor warm" (Revelations); there's no time to stop.
The jeep is useful for bad roads; on good ones it drags and consumes our
whole day's labor.

Oleanders of Lykos. The mountain plateau where Hierapolis (now
Pammukkale = cotton castle), 22 km., lies is striking. As you face the low
plateau the whiteness blinds you; a sugary whiteness broken only by the
red and the green which the oleanders fasten to its slopes. One might
say these slopes are made of petrified cataracts. Here and there the
waters are still running; elsewhere, their chalky sediments have formed

little basins and stairs. At the foot of the mountains a poor village—
Yürüks [nomads] , I think. High up on the plateau the ancient city, Epictetus' hometown. Its theater reminded me of our own theater of Herod
Atticus. Under the theater, says Murray's guide, was the Plutonium, a
deep hole in the earth, wide as a man, whence noxious vapors emerged,
breaths of the kingdom of death.

At the pool near the gymnasium the water gushes out. We undressed and
took a dip; temperature 37°C; the water feels stinging to the eyes. A
beautiful, diaphanous, light green color; at the bottom, reclining marbles
which little by little the lime covers, eroding their shapes away.

As we were swimming a gypsy, gaunt and very dark, came and sat among
the oleanders and started playing his lute; he called it a saz; a few sporadic,
metallic tones darted out, beautiful as butterflies, from the diaphanous
sky.

You must make such trips on foot or on an animal; you must be free.
Otherwise grace catches you for a moment, like the thorn of a bush,
while "schedule" drags you on forcibly. You leave behind a shred of your
clothing in order to continue. You finally return home in tatters.

We were back at Denizli around 11:00. A vain effort to telephone
Ankara to learn what the Ministry had decided about my fate. At 13:00
we started out for Muğla; still women in red dresses. Good road as
far as Tavas. Authorities, etc.; they offered us tea at the café in the
square. Weather about to rain, the road tolerable a while longer, up to
Medetköy. It would be interesting to investigate the architectural geography of Turkey; here are beautiful carved windows and grilles worked in
wood, things of some antiquity. The villagers know of Louis Robert; someone showed me an inscription in the courtyard of his house. They brought
us bronze coins. I bought a small brooch with an engraved horse. (Which
ancient site is this?)

I climbed in next to E. on the truck escorting us; the road started to get
bad. We climbed uphill through Honazdag. We stopped at a small cross-

road, where a superannuated bus was waiting, full of notables from the village that could be seen on our right, its fortress crowning the peak of a high precipice: the Tavaskale. Exquisite sight. It's raining. They invited us up to the village; they had prepared everything; we had no time. They were speaking Turkish; E. said a few vibrant phrases to them in his own language. "Why should I speak French to them?" he remarked; "they won't understand that either." We left via mountain trails; rain, skidding, and abrupt curves; at times there are scarcely two handspans at the edge of the precipice for the car to pass. We preferred to ride in the jeep, which is easier to drive. The road, so they told us, has been abandoned to its fate for years. At times thick pine trunks were in front of us, at times potholes that had to be filled so we could pass. Without the four or five workmen who followed us in the truck we would have had to turn back.

By 19:30 we had descended to the plain. We stopped at the Akçay River; in the distance ahead the stream was swollen; on this side of it there were deep ditches which the peasants had opened up to irrigate the fields (village Armanköy). We needed two or three makeshift bridges for the cars to cross over. Finally we crossed the swollen "çay" (stream) and started uphill again through the pines. It was growing dark.

We couldn't go faster than 10 to 15 km. per hour. Life-giving air, gloomy skies, furrowed every so often by distant flashes of lightning. Then darkness overtook us. For hours only the car headlights lit the forest. A forest butchered in every way a man can imagine. Trees with deep wounds, broken, fallen down; everywhere maimed limbs under the cruel lights of the cars, in the balm of the night and rain. You long to tell them to stop so you can take the uphill road alone. We stopped to rest our numbed bones at a hut, belonging to the forestry service, I imagine. Immense quiet of the mountain, like a good bed; the soft light from the oil lamp of the ranger who came to meet us. We stepped into his humble cabin for a moment. Logs were burning in the fireplace. Evocations from the depths of other times. Through my mind passed the green water of the pool up on Hierapolis, its tepidness, the metallic sound of the gypsy's lute, the oleanders in the limey soil. Of what is our life made?

Two or three colors, two or three sounds govern us more, determine
our fate more than the endless babbling of everyday give and take. Then,
Epictetus again: "If you twist my hand (or foot) a little more you'll
break it." The master twisted it and broke it. "I told you so," he remarked,
just as we speak to a child playing with a piece of glass. In the hands of
his master he felt like something owned.

At 0:30, from the last trail, the lights of Muğla. We stopped—I almost
wrote landed—at the central square, at the feet of the statue of Mustafa
Kemal (173 km.). We went on to a modern concrete building, of Central
European origin: the "Halkevi," the People's House. A small park encircled it. Big glass doors. In the lobby a man, half-awake, politely told us:
"Yes, we have reserved two beds for you; another gentleman is sleeping
in the third; would you have the kindness not to wake him up." He
didn't understand why we refused this state hospitality. We went to the
Ege Oteli, a hotel built around a patio; it doesn't lack charm. A clever
businessman could have built something very attractive, but there's no
demand.

We were hungry; we were exhausted. They showed us a restaurant that
was still open. I asked for fried eggs, but fire is a difficult thing. After
much blowing, two coals were resurrected, but the frying also seemed a
very complicated affair. There's no cheese.

SUNDAY, JUNE 25

At the Ege Oteli the servant, a kind man named Husein, proudly showed
me the bathroom; there was also a tub, but the room was filled to the
ceiling with unused mattresses. From my window, as I was shaving, I saw
the courtyard of a mosque. The electric light switch of my room was
placed outside the door, in the corridor.

We woke up late, around ten. But even today, at this hour, they serve the
cheese with a dropper. How are these people nourished? There must be
some trick we are missing; Muğla is the capital of a province, of a district
that must be large and wealthy, but Turkish provincial cities are shy, as if

they're still veiled. Under the veneer of modern buildings (state buildings mainly), old customs persevere, as best they can.

EVENING. MARMARITSA

We set out from Muğla around noon. A marvelous road, enough to make you weep: pine trees, pine trees, cicadas, and the breath of resin that drives you mad. At the site of Gök Ova, ancient tombs hewn in the sides of the rock. Marmaritsa (so I heard it pronounced in Greek) is a beautiful bay. Ancient name: Physcus (Murray)—in Turkish, Marmaris (opposite Rhodes). The tragedy is that they've turned it into a naval station: it's full of battleships with their radios blaring out passionate songs (amanedes). Here the police chief welcomed us—gold teeth, pistol in his rear pocket; he speaks only Russian, plus three words of French.

Our hotel is above a bare, rectangular hall; they call it the seamen's club; it shelters a multitude of infants. They gave us a room with two beds and, in spite of the heat of this seashore, the traditional quilts. None of the faucets work.

We went downstairs to eat at the club. Instinctively I asked for fish; they were surprised; they brought three sparids, undoubtedly fried the day before yesterday. In the afternoon, a swim in the sea; my first since '47; all right. And now, as it grows dark, amid the ships' radios and the hoarse open-air movie-theater, on the boards of this dock where we are dining, I crave some freshly fried marides*, something less attainable than the daughter of King Kamuz ben Tamuz in the lands of Sin and Masin (Arabian Nights).

MONDAY, JUNE 26. LABRAUNDA, IN MY TENT, EVENING

Yesterday we slept at Marmaris. Early in the morning, back to Muğla; one of E.'s whimsies. We ate around 11:00, then set out for Mylasa. We passed through Yatağan and stopped at Eskihisar; it is the Stratoniceia of

---

*The small fried fish served in the tavernas.

Antiochus Soter. As we enter, goats around an ancient altar. Then, to the ancient theater. I notice my typical reaction on finding myself in the shell of such a theater: I gaze at the distant landscape, always so well chosen, and immediately afterward look about for the spectators, trying to see their eyes; thousands of rows of eyes, riveted on a detail, on a moment that cannot be preserved—not a specific action which I could easily surmise. The eyes together with their emotion fade away, just as stars die, and this empty space is left, so much loneliness . . . We sat down in the village square to have coffee; the villagers surrounded us and offered two small bags of copper coins; I bought a Ptolemaic copper coin. Early in the afternoon we were at Mylasa; in the nearby village, Kargiçak (it means axe, here too a Minoan sign), the mounts were waiting for us near an olive mill—smell of crushed olives. We mounted at 18:15 and took the road uphill to Mount Tmolus.

TUESDAY MORNING

I don't think I've slept like this for years—perhaps not since Poros! Again I rediscover myself, another man. For a moment, the urge of that poem . . .

Yesterday, before I fell asleep in this charming little tent, crickets, dogs, horses' hooves (the path passes alongside), the dialogue of two screech owls, and in the distance frogs; infinite night fragrances.

I moored in a chthonic harbor, here
blood throbs in the pines in the rocks
that seek to relive the embrace . . .
under the walnut tree
the gleam of the axe . . . ,
milk drips from the cut fig,
and the girl branded on the shoulder
for the sacrifice,
the ethereal girl . . .

Yesterday around 20:30 we arrived here at Axel Persson's camp; it was almost dark. As we traveled we often found and lost parts of the ancient road, the villagers passed by us saying "tak-tak," the Swedish greeting they've learned. When we dismounted, Axel took us to see the place he loves best, the sanctuary of Zeus Stratius; Herodotus mentions it (V. 119); I have it with me; Axel knows the passage by heart: "here fell two thousand Persians and ten thousand Carians. Those who escaped from here were overtaken at Labraunda in the sanctuary of Zeus Stratius, a large, sacred grove of plane trees. Only the Carians, as far as we know, offer sacrifices to Zeus Stratius."

The sacred grove still alive with plane trees (among pines and oleanders). The moon was quite large; the marble of the small Ionic temple was alive with the paleness of flesh. A strange feeling, familiar yet unfamiliar, at night, in the breast of this mountain, which they have opened to reveal again these signs of life.

My tent is pitched under a big walnut tree. Sleep overtook me last night as I was looking at a handful of moonlight touching my feet.

Written with a pencil

Without chiton, without lips, without eyes,
lesser kings with comrades and concubines
and whatever the Cretan ship unloaded
down by the shore at Halicarnassus;
high-breasted slave girls taught by snakes
and slim acrobats taught by the bull,
so much merchandise
and merchants with the accounts of the Labyrinth.
Without chiton, without lips, without eyes,
all beg to be stripped of earth,
they wish it
even upon these slopes
exposing so many breasts to the moon,
and this man who leaned to rest
against the pillar of the epigonoi,

hearing with closed eyelids, crickets and frogs
digging.

AFTERNOON

ΙΔΡΙΕΥΣ ΕΚΑΤΟΜΝΩ ΜΥΛΑΣΕΥΣ
ΑΝΕΘΗΚΕ ΤΟΥΣ ΟΙΚΟΥΣ ΔΙΙ ΛΑΜΒΡΑΝΔΩ*

In the morning Axel showed me the excavation site in detail. Idrieus was
the brother of Mausolus; when Mausolus settled in Halicarnassus, Idrieus
stayed at Mylasa as king of Caria (351–347).

Lesser kings, intriguers, who had organized a sybaritic life around the
worship of Zeus Labraunda in these communes (exclusive clubs) still
seen next to the temple.

Axel says that under these buildings (middle of the third century B.C.)
are traces of an older, sixth-century temple. The great prevalence in these
parts of the axe in place names and representations makes him think he
might find bilingual monuments that would allow him to read the Minoan
script.

The archaeological team working here is marvelously organized. The
greater part of its financial means are provided by private contributions;
Swedish shops give them discounts, and Swedish ships transport them
for free. The team consists of Persson at the head, who goes around
tirelessly with a big black umbrella; his wife, a doctor, who protects him
from the sun, fatigue, and everything else (she also provides the workers
and nearby villagers with medical care); and about ten young men, all
Swedes except one (a Dane), full of spirit and eagerness. Two women,
Karen Leman, Persson's assistant, and the petite Marianne, wife of Lars
the architect—my neighbors at the camp.

At noon the subprefect who had escorted us from Mylasa arrived with a
long snake; he killed it with his pistol as it reached down to drink water.

*Idrieus, son of Hecatomnus, from Mylasa / dedicated the houses to Zeus Labradeus.

WEDNESDAY. IN MY TENT AFTER SIESTA

Enjoyable bath up there at the spring before breakfast.

We're leaving tomorrow; I'm on the verge of tears; I could stay here a month.

From 7 A.M. on I watched the excavations, took photographs, saw them restoring a piece from an Ionic pillar. How much lighter than myths are these Hellenistic remains!

EVENING

After lunch we went with Axel and his wife to Tsopan's cabin. He's the only man who remains in these parts after the excavation season; even the nearby village is deserted in the winter months. He stays to guard the expedition property. "Tsopan Police Axel," he would say every so often; that is, "I, Tsopan, am Axel's guard." He made coffee and served us two at a time because he only had one pair of demitasses. A short little man with excellent mimetic skills, very useful because none of us knew enough Turkish to talk to him. He brought to my mind the mannerisms of the villagers in our parts. Thus, with gestures and inarticulate sounds he acted out for us his winter life, alone with the wild beasts of the mountain. Axel says he is an excellent dancer of phallic dances; I was unable to see them because it was Ramazan.

In the afternoon great excitement at the excavations: they had found an altar with a horse in bas-relief. We called that day the day of the horse. Strange what enlightenment a discovery brings, this sudden ray of light.

THURSDAY, JUNE 29

The horses and the sun behind us—rhythm.

We're going down to the shore at Halicarnassus.

We left Labraunda at 8:00. Axel with his walking stick, came together with his wife, as far as the rock of farewell, as he calls it, a high stone prow over the footpath. I turned and looked once more at the magnanimous old man, dressed in white, waving with his right hand. I still could hear his pronunciation of " . . . Zeus Labraunda." His voice was emotional, like his hands when they touched the marbles. I heard him talking about the voyages of the Minoans, about the commerce they must have had with these parts . . . My mind kept returning to the bards who sang, among a world of refugees, the glories of the Trojan War. Will he have the good fortune to find the Minoan messages he seeks? He's one of the few left us from the old European tradition—God help him.

On the road to our right about twenty-five wild boars climbing fiercely uphill; our guides started shouting. Below Kargiçak, Yusuf was waiting for us with the car. We saw briefly the Frankish fortress and a Greco-Roman(?) arch with the double-axe in bas-relief; right after lunch we took the road to Halicarnassus. A bad road; it took two and a half hours.

Pine woods, cicadas, resin-scented wind, sea breeze. There's the sea!

Visit to the subprefect's; the judge came too. They'll provide hospitality for us in the Municipality. E.'s room must be the mayor's office. Mine opens on a big hall—that of the city council, I imagine. The mountains of Kos are clearly visible. In the streets many speak Greek: Cretan Turks; about a thousand souls have been settled in the Greek quarter. You hear them as they pass by: "Hi, Ibrahim, how's your Mom?"

The church of the Christians, destroyed. Animal skins, one black, hang from the closed entrance; it once was a movie house, they told us. There's something cruel in this travesty of churches—better to demolish them. Not that we don't do the same with mosques.

We visited the Frankish fortress of the Crusaders, the "Bodrum" they call it now, an impressive building. A young English-speaking Turk accompanies us. We swam there. On the walls of the fortress shields, lions, and lilies are carved. On the lintel of a big door:

SALVA NOS DOMINE VIGILANTES
CUSTODI NOS DORMIENTES

on another lintel:

F. CORNELIUS DE HABROUCI
CAPITANEUS—1518

Phallic flowers with red heads in the large courtyard of the fortress, the
guard calls them "poisonous fish." The loveliest sky. Herodotus of
Halicarnassus was a subject of the Great King, now that I think of it.

At night we ate at the Kulübü (the club), by the seashore. The harbormaster came too, a kind man, and we arranged for tomorrow's voyage to
Kos. The waiter, another Cretan Turk, is named Husein. The first time
on this tour that we enjoyed a meal.

FRIDAY, JUNE 30

At dawn we set out for Kos by launch. Eleven or twleve miles, two and a
half hours; we also hoisted the sail. Crew: Mustafa from Crete, Mustafa
from Kos, and a kollitiri. The first had served in the Greek army for
seven years. He remembers tales of that time and his officer's "mantenuta"
[mistress] . "I saw her one day in bed," he says, "and I was trapped, a
beautiful woman." When we moored at the island, a marine guard with
inflated bureaucratic rhetoric: "You must go through health inspection."
"My good man, what are you saying, we've come just for a few hours, here
are our passports." But he was insistent; finally the harbormaster came
and released us. I breathed again. That young man kept glancing at us with
such fierce spite that I thought we might spend all our time in some
lazaretto.

Asklepeion; wide terraces; its Italian restorations did not convince me.
Roman house: mosaic fishes, carnations. Museum: Hermaphrodite; small,
high breasts, more feminine than Aphrodite. Short, round urns, the

sarcophagi of small children. The impression that the babies were moving in their mothers' wombs.

We ate at the restaurant. At the next table educators: women and men; occasional crumbs from their talk. I wonder, with awe, how they teach the children. However, a different atmosphere here—vivacity—although rough at times.

17:30 we are back at Halicarnassus. We started again for Yatağan. Misunderstanding: we gave up the plan to continue at night toward Söke. We slept again at Muğla.

SATURDAY, JULY 1

Early from Muğla to Eskiçine; a beautiful little old mosque. Oleanders. Noon at Aydin. Then Söke. Once when I was very young I had come here to see the Bishop of Cheimoniou. All I remember are some stairs in the Bishopric and chained convicts at the dark railroad station; I couldn't recognize a thing. This is a district where antique dealers ask fantastic sums from the stranger. Kuşadasi; the village seems deserted; many houses closed, as if uninhabited. We swam near some huts farther down; here too they speak Greek. Samos is opposite. I begin to feel that our trip has become exhaustingly rapid; the eye can't grasp anything as we pass.

As it grows dark, Ephesus. I don't want to see anything anymore; we're breathless. The only thing I've retained, totally inexplicable, is this inscription: "The statue with the pedestal and the satyr on it was dedicated during the time of the proconsul Rouson."

Then toward Smyrna: familiar air, familiar appearance of the countryside, and the aroma of herbs. Then, little by little from within, the city so well-known to memory, and so strange now, returns to my mind. My God, what am I doing here!

We climbed down to the Tüccar Kulübü (Commercial Club, formerly the Sporting Club.) Our house once stood back here.

Saturday evening. There was dancing below. Jews, they told us at our table; later they added that they've taken the place of the Greeks in Smyrna.

After dinner, a few steps toward the location of our house: the nothing-ness. And still a few more steps toward the "Ke" (quay).

You can spell out faded letters with difficulty. I am somewhere else. As though to return me to my senses, the diplomat accompanying me whispered: "The Greeks say the Turks burned Smyrna; the Turks say the Greeks burned it. Who can know which is the truth?" I'm not in the mood for talk.

Just as if one night
you happened to enter
the city that reared you,
and later they razed it to the ground and rebuilt it,
and you struggle to transpose older times
to recognize again . . .

SUNDAY, JULY 2

The sea at dawn from my window, and the rocks known as the Two Brothers; that was all. I remembered the burial urns of Kos. Smyrna must be such an urn for me—no one can return. Like a ghost, Smyrna has lost its shadow.

At 8 A.M. we started for Vourla. Skala is a forbidden zone, the authorities at Ankara had informed us. But yesterday our companion (from the Road Service) said spontaneously that we could swim there. In these parts you cannot depend on anyone's information.

From the Konak, with the clock tower in front of it, we took the familiar road toward Kokaryali and beyond. I tried to recognize my uncle's house, but didn't succeed. Although I had gone to bed at two o'clock and gotten up at five, I did not feel any fatigue; memory was working with absolute

precision: It was as though I had been away from these parts no more than
a year.

We came out on the "cartroad" for Vourla (now called Urla). Some Sunday
traffic. The shape of the fortress for an instant; then the farm of St.
George—two or three huts in the old days. Here we used to stop the carts
to rest and have a snack. Now it is a much more important settlement,
but it seems to have maintained its old way-station tradition.

The changes do not bother me today as they did yesterday in transformed
Smyrna. My whole being is tied to Skala's face. This weighs more heavily
on me; I am a dedicated participant in a magic rite which I do not understand. I know that a crisis will occur, whose consequences I cannot
reckon; that I have prepared myself for it carelessly; that perhaps I have
done something like provoking the dead or violating the nature of things—
a shameless act.

It's too late to turn back; the machinery has been set in motion: I am
tied to the thread of this shore, which is being wound by someone on the
other end, steadily, inexorably. But the wind, the color, the sky, are
imperishable, victorious; you don't know if your eye is seeing or is
groping.

A state of twilight of the mind beneath the everyday stereotyped reactions.
As we passed the Sivrihisar road (the sign said "Seferi Hissar"), my friend
roused me to ask whether the place name had any relation to my name.
We made the forty kilometers to Skala in about an hour.

For a moment, it seemed strange that the morning's north wind was still
blowing from the same direction; that the islands, St. Marcella, Jannos,
were in the same place; tiny Monopetro seemed more sunken. I exclaimed
their names to E., trying to describe to him the subterranean cave under
the fig tree on the island of St. John. He seemed to show some interest
only when he heard the word "Clazomenae." Then I felt how little
knowledge of archaeology I really have.

As always, the incredible occurred suddenly: the jeep stopped and we got out at Skala, a little past the old fountain, on the right side of the paved road heading toward Vourla.

So we found ourselves on the road parallel to the shorefront, which separated my grandmother's garden from the backyards of our houses. We turned toward the sea: no calmness but a nightmarish stillness. The landscape was the inside of a sphere; and the things enclosed in that sphere, myself with them, were continually diminishing and shrinking and disintegrating, until they became a crumpled, rough sketch of the past, forgotten on a shelf.

The wooden "ship's gangplank" is no longer there; but I was surprised that five or six of its thick poles still remained. The arcades of Batis' cafe are standing, and the buildings over them. Then,.a few things I don't recognize. Then, our "little house."

The panes of the ground floor windows broken, the iron door terribly rusted: it can't have been painted since we lived there. I still have the key in Athens. Michael Bougas, who was looking after the house at the time of the catastrophe, gave it to me in '34. It was the only thing he salvaged, along with the lives of his wife and his children, when he managed to flee from pursuit on a raft. The shutters of the upper storey are rotted; they looked as though they could never be closed. The walls were leprous. I tried to peer through to the inside of the house; I discerned the glass partition in the dining room, but there wasn't enough light to see further. While we were taking photographs, two or three children slipped through the rusted door like big rats.

To the left, as we faced the "little house," a soldier was watching and studying us curiously. To the right, the shop that once separated us from grandmother's house had been demolished. Ours is the only cared-for one amid this numbed retinue of disabled dwellings. Its old arcades with the two thick pillars have been replaced by some thin poles, and a whole second storey has been added. It must be the headquarters of some important person now; I didn't see a soul there, but an automobile shrouded in a white cover was moored outside. I strolled around, walking along the breakwater of the harbor as far as the lighthouse, now white-washed, looking as though made of salt. The old houses at the base of the breakwater still stand. I also recognized two or three of the short poles where they used to tie the caiques, and an old rusted cannon used for the same purpose; at that time they said it came from the battle of Çeşme.*

There at the sea's edge, beside the lighthouse, I suddenly turned my back to the houses, which were staring at me like sick animals. It was almost as though the little life still left in them depended on me alone. I looked toward my islands; the sea terribly alive and the wind seeking to reunite it with the face of a dead girl. Poor Skala.

I was unable to go to Kalamakia; they wouldn't permit it. I returned by the back road. Blinded windows. The iron brackets that supported Aunt Ellie's balcony point directly to an exit into the void. But all around the feeling that everything is terribly shrunken. Uncle Kokos' small living room is there: rows of bricks painted deep red from that time. In place of the garden gate they've put the old main door from the front of the house; I recognized it from the wicket in its door. At our house the buildings back out are still standing; here too, everything is closed. I was unable to find my initials, which I had carved on a wall with the trowel when I was ten.

On the other side of the road, the front part of Grandmother's garden has become a public park. Its eucalyptus trees are still breathing, aged and thin; its three ponds in fine shape, with water and goldfish. The "Octagulari"† seems to have been turned into something dreadfully official. Its iron stairs are gone; they have blocked its windows, and a sign with the crescent hangs over its ground floor door. I wasn't interested in asking for a translation of what it says. There, when very small, I saw for the first time a ship's compass, left from a sailing ship once owned by my

*The battle of Çeşme, west of Smyrna, was fought on July 5, 1770, during the Turkish-Russian wars. The entire force of Turkish ships was destroyed by the Russian fleet.
†That's what it was always called (a borrowed word from French or Italian, I suppose). It was a two-story octagonal tower, rural in type, in the style of the last century, one room on each floor, usually unoccupied.—G. S.

grandfather. This nautical implement exercised a mysterious attraction on me as if it were an instrument of alchemy. I examined it so persistently that, in the end, it finally fell into bits and pieces.

Beyond the garden I was surprised that the wheel-well still drew water; a very tiny donkey was turning it. The mulberry tree that shaded it is still alive, but beyond this, chaos: neither vineyards nor olive trees nor pomegranate trees nor fig trees—a wasteland. On the other side, to the right, the most conspicuous absence: the old plane tree has died, that huge tree bustling with sparrows in the afternoons. Our church, St. Nicholas,*·has been turned into a school. (I see my mother, the silver icon of the Virgin in her arms, going there every August 15.) Something remains of the houses across from it, where Stephanis Simionis, our boatman, used to live.

Once more to the pier. Three sleeping boats in the little harbor that was once a beehive. I said "Merhaba"† to the man staring at one of them. He answered, "Merhaba." He, two soldiers, and the little kids I saw sneaking out of our house were the sole population of the harbor of Skala.

We headed on toward Vourla. In other times I often rode my bicycle over this same road. The long, high wall that fenced the vineyards, the sentry-box, the iron windmill no longer exist. The hills to the right, naked; out of ten mills, a few ruins.

We had coffee at the square; I absolutely could not recognize a thing. We asked if we could go over to St. John's Island; I was lucky. A guard of the lazaretto happened to be right there and he phoned the doctor, who agreed to allow it. We crossed in the jeep along the causeway built all the way out to the island. The doctor's brother-in-law, a tanner from Smyrna,

*It was dedicated to the Vourliot neo-martyr Nectarius, but people called it: "St. Nicholas the Martyr" or "St. Nicholas." When I read Mr. Melioris' fine book, the stories about the life of the saint told by the local people in my childhood were relived in my memory. (See Nikos E. Melioris, Ta Vourla tis Mikras Asias, part I, History, pp. 325 ff., Athens, 1951.)—G. S.
†A Turkish greeting: Good day! How are you?

was also vacationing there for the summer. He spoke French and German. He had studied in Germany during the First World War; he remembered Greek fellow students: "We starved a lot in those years," he said. We swam together. He advised us not to swim far out because of the savage fish.

They showed us a few traces of old mosaics; I picked up a few stones. The guard was holding two or three bronze Roman coins, very worn, which he had found there. "There's a 'yiasma' [holy place] —they use the same word in Turkish as in Greek—he added, "which has a long underground tunnel that comes out on the mainland, they say, way off at the mountain." I knew he was talking about the subterranean cave, the chapel of the Saint of the "Paroxymon."* In my day people used to say the tunnel led to the miracle-performing Virgin at Vourla. You can discard the gods sometimes, but the rituals of worship do not go away so easily. Little remains of the fig tree where little votive rags used to be tied. I climbed down: small arches carved in the rock, and the altar tiles still blackened from the candles of the other world.

As I emerged I understood how Lot's wife turned into a pillar of salt when she looked back.

Around 13:30 we were at Kokaryali (restaurant Grosse Marie or Soula). After much rushing around in Smyrna, for it was growing dark, 19:35, to Pergamum. A five-hour road, bearable. A quick visit to the Asklepieion and then to the acropolis (6 kilometers from the city). How can the mind grasp so many things;—useless without fresh sensations. I admire my companion who finds time and mood to read Baedeker, too. We returned by night. At the front door of the hotel a valet, a type straight out of the movies, welcomed us. They gave E. a room with bath; the bath of course didn't work.

The dark blue houses of Pergamum in the July twilight.

MONDAY, JULY 3

A quick look at the Museum.

*As they used to call the malaria fevers; from the word paroxysm.—G. S.

ΠΕΡΙΘΥΤΗΣ ΚΑΙ ΘΕΡΑΠΕΥΤΗΣ*

reads one marble: who now serves us?

And at the very bottom of the inscription a Silenus mocks you, sticking out his tongue.

At 9:00, Ayvalik. I counted three Christian churches; the crescent on the belfry of one. I didn't happen to know this land before, but I can easily imagine its life in other days—at the shore, in the arched alleys, and in the houses, with pillars at the doors—Ionian, Doric, Corinthian—our own houses which now look numb.

I asked for a card to send to Athens; it was impossible, although I asked in many shops. The only ones I found showed skiers on the Ulu Dağ; Turkey shows only her Europeanization. I finally hit on some local photographs the size of visiting cards and mailed them.

In these parts you cannot help but recall constantly the old Hellenism. Four or five archaeological periods in Asia Minor: Preclassical, Classical, Hellenistic, Byzantine—and the Neohellenic.This last one you snatch just as it is sinking into the ground. You can still discern the umbilical cords that tie it to the world above and are severed one after another. Greek language, churches, houses, traditional gestures; after two generations it all will have been extinguished. And now, for how many people do they still exist? I said to a foreigner: "I saw three Christian churches." The reply: "There are many factories here." He's a foreigner, but what about my dear compatriots?

Leaving Ayvalik the road passes through endless olive groves. You travel through miles of the trees. At the port of Burhaniye we swam at an inhospitable sandy shore. The natives will need a long time to become used to the sea. They have it, but, imagine, they don't know what to do with it! The small harbors left behind by the Greeks are empty. The same could be said about the middle class. In the old days the Turkish middle class consisted of Greeks, Armenians, or Jews; they were the

*Sacrificer and servant to the gods.

masters (pashas, beys) or farmers. The middle class here is just now forming; but it has no tradition. One sees this in provincial hotels, which are rapidly being reduced to inns.

Up at Burhaniye I had some soup; it poisoned me badly. At nightfall the road followed the shores of the Appolonia Lake. After the bridge we stopped at the Iziz Han; superb architecture this old han; two fireplaces in the middle, with four pillars each. Now it is used as a sheepfold. Outside the weather has turned gray. We slept at Bursa.

TUESDAY, JULY 4

We were at our homes at 22:30, having covered 2,876 km.

JULY*

> Salva Nos Vigilantes
> (Bodrum)

Such sky, sweet sky, and on the walls
carved lilies, shields, lions, and
Salva Nos Domine Vigilantes
Custodi Nos Dormientes
on the lintel of the door.
In the large courtyard
insolent red flowers
called poisonous fish.
The herald left, showing golden heels,
heels and thighs the color of goldstone.
And the besieged man, alone, shut in;
thirst; the castle is bolted.
Wretched bodies, and the lances of the enemies draw near,
and sleeplessness.
Down at Halicarnassus . . .

*The days 14, 15, and 16 of July, which originally belonged here, I have used for my essay Tris Imeres sta Monastiria tis Kappadokias [Three Days at the Monasteries of Cappadocia] , (editions of the French Institute in Athens, number 78, 1953).—G. S.

To kiss your neck
and my sweat to trickle on the nipples of your breasts,
nipples like tiny red peppers.
It was the eve of the Twelve Apostles
when her carnations spilled over the sand,
and she, sobbing all night,
swimming in shallow grief;
he heard her entangled in her intricate ornaments
like a circus gladiator in the net;
ferocious hands.
Such sky,
and the copper light of the moon
in the garden with the huge cacti
the all-naked moon
and the sea made of skin and wind,
how it breathed.
Poisonous fish like a tale of Herodotus,
golden heels, the lances gleam in the sun;
Salva·Nos Vigilantes—as for sleep
they speak of an ornate grave
very near us.

SUNDAY, AUGUST 13

A capital city that doesn't look after its hinterland, that is indifferent to
its borders, becomes a province; this is what my recent trips have shown.
In this sense I see provincialism in today's hydrocephalic Athens, indulging
herself only in the present and scarcely looking to the past.

SATURDAY, AUGUST 26. CONSTANTINOPLE

Smyrna has lost its shadow; Constantinople still keeps it; one longs for
this in roofless Anatolia. The hotel here (Pera Palace) is what Constantinople needs: relics of the old luxury about to collapse.

Our window faces the Golden Horn, where the sun set. Now on the sea, fine leaden tones. In the foreground the peeling dome of a contemporary building. In front of the dome (at a second-storey window) a man in pajamas "lies in wait"; suddenly he lowers a basket. The vegetable man is below; he drops in a bunch of vegetables. The man pulls up the line swiftly, as if the fish had bit, and closes the window quickly. A spectacle I saw many times in the streets of Constantinople. These men with baskets give me the impression of prisoners.

"I never saw such a thing in my age (i.e., in my life)," said the chauffeur yesterday; he's a Constantinopolite.

SUNDAY, AUGUST 27

I've been thinking fearfully that when we return to Ankara we'll have to stay in the hotel; since the end of July we have no longer had a home; we dismantled everything, waiting for orders from day to day. For three months now, we've been in motion, yet we don't know where we're going. You write; but you don't know whether or not they read your letters. We hear rumors and make plans for cities which most probably we will never see. We have become a factory of tension. How can one work like this? It's not right—so much time in vain.

Need for aimless sightseeing; we went out into the streets and ended up at Hagia Sophia. The Museum, as they call it now, opens on Sundays at one. Thus, I had enough time to study its outside appearance; not from the side we now enter, but from the west, the main entrance, now closed. In front of it much refuse, but it is the only part that can give an idea, even very dim, of the church's facade.

A new surprise each time I enter the great monastery: this tender breathing of space.

They have hung again the big round shields with their Muslim calligraphy. "They are the works of great calligraphers," Ramazanoglu had explained. "We tried to take them out; they wouldn't fit through the doors; we hung them up again so as not to destroy them." Constantinople's Byzantine monuments are in the hands of this man. These green and gold works are so striking and so marvelously placed that there is not even one corner from which you can look without meeting their curves cutting like a saw the lines of the splendid edifice.

Hagia Sophia is, above all, the expanse and soaring of space under the dome, a spaciousness of lines that breathe. The green and gold shields cut and chop up these lines, these soarings, as if they were the wheels that tortured St. Catherine.

Near these, "which wouldn't fit through the doors," the small shields as well as the long, narrow ones were kept and hung up again toward the side of the altar; and there were Turkish banners too. Since the last time I saw the church a systematic Muslim restoration has taken place, insulting to any man who reveres great monuments of art.

SUNDAY, SEPTEMBER 3

St. Theodore of Tyron. "In Byzantine times he was called the Revealer" (Camisi Kilise). In this quarter stood the house of Niketas Choniatis, which was burned down in 1204 (Latins). Vivid mosaics in the narthex. On the right dome a superb Holy Virgin with the child surrounded in the spherical triangles by the Kings of Israel. In the central dome the Apostles. When we visited the church it was a voting center for municipal elections; they took us for voters.

MONDAY, SEPTEMBER 4

Constantinople: on one hand the aged city, and on the other incredible bursts of frenzied native fanaticism. The future is obvious.

WEDNESDAY, OCTOBER 11. PARK PALACE, ANKARA

As of yesterday we have been in this hotel a month. Misery. The men on top "say" we're going to London; the service "says" we're going to Alexandria—words that reach us down here. No answer whatsoever to my letters. And yet, under the conditions that have been created there's no margin left for us to face another winter in Ankara.*

Last Thursday I finished and mailed <u>Cappadocia</u>. Much effort to concentrate amid this hairpulling, and in this temporary room in an Ankara hotel.

FRIDAY, OCTOBER 13. IN THE TRAIN

We left Ankara at 14:45, and have just passed Yenidoğan (16:45).
This indescribable color of Anatolia, the most neutral I've known; the color of a white sheet you've dragged through the mud and left to dry; with it the yellow of autumn grass, a yellow of dumb madness.

We arrive in Smyrna tomorrow afternoon; I preferred this slow-moving train, primarily because it gives me an interim, a no-man's-land, which isolates me from the drones at the office.

SUNDAY, OCTOBER 15, EVENING

TÜCCAR KULÜBÜ, SMYRNA

We didn't arrive in the afternoon, as they had said, but at ten-thirty at night; it's always impossible to get correct information. The last hours, in darkness, were beyond belief. But I don't regret having taken the train. I'm pleased to have seen, as I wanted to, the entrance into Ionia from the Anatolian plateau, more clearly than last June with the jeep. Entering the plains of the Lykos and Maeander Rivers, I found again, a foothold—the psychological one and the other.

MONDAY, OCTOBER 16

I couldn't continue last night; overwhelming need for sleep; I lay down right after dinner. The nightmare of Ankara is gone. From the big window of our room, the sea and the whole amphitheater of the Gulf of Smyrna

*Seferis was transferred to London as Embassy Counselor in May 1951.

from the Two Brothers to the Bay of Bornova. I look, I keep looking, insatiably. I find it very natural that I left these parts for Attica. They have great affinity: the same atmosphere, the same myth; even the gods seem to look down on you with the same sort of disposition.

Although I had known since last June that not even a stone remained, I went again to the place I know our house theoretically is. Afterward I wandered for hours through the streets.

I've memorized the map of Smyrna from an 1898 English guidebook.* I'm trying to apply this to both the ruined and the new buildings before me. I lie on my side on the beach and spread it out; then I abandon myself to the sorcery of memory. I think it was Alexandria which was compared to a cloak. Smyrna too is a cloak spread out as far as the castle of Pagus. Except that the whole center has been burned; the outskirts remain, and a huge pit which they have tried to patch with trees, kiosks, and other things with the plasticity of cement, and wide boulevards that lead you to the despair of the roads of Giorgio de Chirico.

From our house I found myself suddenly at the Central School for Girls, one of the very few old buildings that have survived. As far as I can recall, in my day the two neighborhoods were some distance apart. You had to wind through alley after alley, see many windows and many faces, pass through so much life—in order to get from one to the other. Now, among these empty, intersecting streets, one stride seems enough; all the proportions have changed for me. You still pass by the burned debris (left by the fire of 1922*) and piles of dirt which look like offal from the crude sprouting of reinforced concrete. And it seems only yesterday that the great ship was wrecked. I feel not hatred; what prevails within me is the opposite of hatred: an attempt to comprehend the mechanism of catastrophe.

*It was Murray's Handbook: Asia Minor, Transcaucasia, Persia (London, Sanford). —G. S.
*On August 27, 1922, the Turkish irregulars entered Smyrna, burnt it to the ground, and summarily executed the Greeks and the other Christians who had not fled from the city.

Later we headed toward the outskirts of the cloak, where you can still make out the lines which have survived on the worn-out cloth. There existed a peculiar Smyrnian rococo; you see it while walking along the seafront: balconies, ornaments, iron doors, interior layouts. Rich houses of other times, built with good workmanship of solid materials for generations of children and grandchildren to enjoy them. Now they are inhabited by people who hide as though frightened, unfamiliar, behind half-open doors, or peer through windows. In the back streets, beyond "Parallel" Street, the balconies are asleep. Only from one, the oldest, they were lowering worn-out furniture with ropes: this decay without resurrection. Here's something that was accepting the devastation.

TUESDAY, OCTOBER 17

You wake up, draw the curtains, and are astonished by St. Demetrius' sea. As you are shaving you see in the mirror a big ship heading straight toward you; you think it will enter your room. Familiarity begins anew: it is your land, but there is also something more biological, more primitive in this attraction of your land—something like the magnetism of fire to ice, like hunger, and like desire. I have never before felt this sensation, in the same way.

Yet I reflected, as I woke up this morning, this climate would be un-healthy, if I lived, as once I had planned, for some time in Smyrna. At every step memories stir within me overwhelmingly; a constant, almost nightmarish piling up of images; incessant invitations from the dead, so many dead branches of the family tree. I can't imagine this process stopping, even if I served here for two or three years. Everything pulls me backward. At this moment, as I put down my pen, I identify with the twelve-year-old child who opened a notebook for the first time to write his diary. The violet ink, the spelling mistakes in the carefully penned title, the mood of the room, the mood of the day—all hit me like a handful of buckshot. One can stand such an intense state of mind without going mad for no more than a few days.

It is better this way. This stay in Smyrna closes a cycle that started in the last years of my childhood. From now on there's neither starting point nor arrival; the world exists here or there, as the world goes, and one gets nowhere.

WEDNESDAY, OCTOBER 18

Yesterday was the second day I've been occupied with professional stupidities. Fortunately, the days are marvelous; at noon we ate outdoors at Kokargyali, by the edge of the sea, two whole hours of light. As we were returning I picked out my uncle's house.

Around dusk at the warehouse of S. Bey, the Smyrniot wholesale merchant of figs and currants; he's richer in spirit than by profession. I met him during my trip here last July and felt great liking for him.

Once a foreign fellow-diplomat, traveling for his country's commercial interests, met him on business. When they had finished, S. asked: "Tell me, please, who's the Prince of Aquitaine?"

The other, after going through various genealogies, admitted his surprise: "Well, how come you are interested in this prince?"

"He's in Eliot's Waste Land."

"What about Eliot?"

"Let me explain. I read once in a foreign newspaper:

Mr. Eugenides, the Smyrna merchant
Unshaven, with a pocketful of currants . . .*

What does this wretch mean insulting us, us Smyrniot currant merchants, I thought. I wrote immediately to London to send me Eliot's books."

He received the books and became a fan of the poet.

*T. S. Eliot, The Complete Poems and Plays, 1909-1950 (New York, 1971), p. 43.

In July he told me that he approves of Eliot's position: Anglo-Catholic in religion, royalist in politics, classic in literature. I asked—but there was no time for him to answer—how these precepts could be translated into modern Mohammedan and Turkish terminology. He was a Popular Party candidate for Parliament in the last elections.

At any rate S.'s warehouse is the liveliest place I've seen so far in Turkey. It stands behind the harbor. It was growing dark as I turned into the narrow alley. Out of the big door poured a heavy stream of workers who had just quit for the day; many women, some with baggy pants. Inside was dim light, the feverish pulse of machines; it is the height of the fig export season. An old building, it could very well have been exactly the same eighty years ago. The stairs, corridors, and passages to places where the figs are packed are like a labyrinth. I climbed the wide wooden steps; an employee led me to the office, passing through a glassed-in veranda. S. was talking with a one-armed English agent, disabled in the First World War, about ships and tonnage of cargoes; like a cabalistic symbol, "The Silver Ocean" kept recurring in the conversation. It must have been the name of the expected ship.

I sat down while they were talking, and looked around. Too much patina and many dark corners. A room somehow haunted. Safes for money. A bench covered with various papers, many glasses, and a big bottle of water; beside it a fan, the latest model. Wires hanging from the ceiling; some with electric bulbs fastened to them, others loose. Various foremen came in, asked questions, received brief answers, and left. Every so often telephones would ring. The subject was always the day a ship would be arriving or quantities of cargoes. Behind me on the bookshelves, various English books, most of them poetry. In a handy place The Family Reunion. During a pause, S. asked me in the same tone of voice he used in speaking about "The Silver Ocean": "Why did Eliot stop using choruses after this play?"

Then he gave me William Plomer's poem "The Levant," in the anthology of the World's Classics, to read. The poem didn't move me especially, but he seemed to admire it.

The one-armed Englishman had left. We talked a little more; the telephones never stopped; always about ships that were arriving.

"Yes, the cargo will be ready. We'll work nights, too."

I thought of the tranquil fig trees I had seen as it was growing dark on the Maeander Plain. I imagined the life cycle of a fig, from its birth on: the webs of interests and feelings it encounters, not forgetting sycophancies.*
This pattern of thinking led me easily into the mechanism of life of the ancient harbors of Asia Minor. Ships, cargoes, harbors, crowded cities, persecutions, migrations, refugees, over and over again.—"οἴη περ καρπῶν γενεή . . . "†

I felt this was not the right time for a relaxed discussion or for Eliot's choruses. To conclude the visit, I asked where one could get good figs. "They are in the market," he said, "we only export them."

But he rang a bell and spoke to someone in Turkish. After a while the same man brought a small cellophane bag with about twenty figs wrapped in flowered papers. "Look, there's this one here, my competitor."

I took out a pencil to jot down the name. As if he had not noticed, he unwrapped the figs carefully and spread them out in front of him. Then he opened them one by one and examined them. The honey color of the opened fruits, the multicolored golden papers, gave a New Year's aura to his gestures in the dim electric light. "I think this packet isn't so bad. Out of twenty-four figs, five spoiled."

He rang the bell again, and, when they brought another small bag, started the same meticulous task. "Ours are better," he said. "I think I can offer you a few. "However," he added smiling, " 'that man' "—and he pointed

*Sycophancy (fig-revealing), is the art of false accusation, false witness, and slander. This word of obscure origin and multiple meanings, coined in Athens in the sixth century B.C., signified the behavior of a sycophant—one who accused the illegal exporters of figs or brought hidden figs into light or prosecuted others to extort money by blackmail or false accusations.
†"as is the generation of fruit . . . "

in the direction where the man who had brought the small bag had disappeared—"is very sly; he must have picked our best packet."

"You are the Dr. Faustus of the fig business," I told him.

And he, laughing: "I like keeping up the traditions of the East. You know, we have a custom of kissing children's hands to demonstrate to them our happiness. A few days ago I couldn't restrain myself and I kissed the hand of an American."

"And how old was that American?"

"Oh, about thirty-five."

THURSDAY, OCTOBER 19

Yesterday we climbed and walked around the Castle of Pagus. At noon we ate nearby; the restaurant is owned by Cretan Turks. They speak, as they all do, wonderful Greek; they feel great nostalgia for their island. I remember the shoemaker from Ankara whom everybody called a grouch and a complainer. As soon as I said to him in Cretan dialect "How are you, pal?" he calmed down.

We strolled down through the narrow alleys. I don't remember anything about this quarter. I'm surprised that it doesn't interest me; my whole life here is absorbed by the workings of memory; and light—I drink it insatiably.

A little before lunch I asked to be directed to the place where St. Photina's once stood. Ruins; the capriciousness of ruins; like London during the blitz. I'm constantly haunted by those dark blue flowers sprouting from the wreckage. Only fragments of standing walls still mark the place of the old Greek Cathedral. Somewhere you can make out the initials B.S. of the nearby Bank of Salonika. Then they showed me the site of my grandmother's house, the "Berhane" [large, rambling house] : a park has swallowed up everything, like the sea. I shall not have courage to return to Skala. One does not make such trips twice.

Early in the afternoon to Boutza in Pelagonia; we stayed until late in the evening. The dull despair of an old villa.

SATURDAY, OCTOBER 21, EPHESUS

Ephesus, old Ayasuluk (Hagios Theologos), is now called Selçuk. Down in the village, in the little museum, are some Greco-Roman statues. Insignificant, but you find the sense of touch present somehow, and this is something: a naked torso, the statue of another Aphrodite seated, endless folds in her chiton. Eros on her knees; the child's palm pressing her breast has survived (the rest of the hand is broken); a sensual maternity.

The nuisance of not knowing the language; the guard who accompanied us speaks only Turkish and seems to be bored with everything. And explanations written only in Turkish; nationalistic stubbornness.

First thing in Ephesus, the city of Lysimachus, I looked for the old harbor. The map shows it as a reclining bottle with a very long, narrow neck, ending at the Cayster River, with its base leaning against the border of Arkadiani. We took this route. The day after a rain; the wet stones of the broad avenue glistened. Moldings with sculptured marble flowers scattered over the ground. A rare thing: you heard the smell from the cyclamen. We went on. Opposite us was the hill with the small building called "St. Paul's Prison." The proud road vanishes into bulrushes and reeds: the remaining seaweed of the old harbor. As for the sea, the silt carried down by the Cayster has moved it far away. On our right are the baths; in front of us the barking of sheep dogs; in the distance, as far as the horizon, the absolute solitude of the plain.*

*"The plain [of Ayasolük] is extensively cultivated by the Greeks of Kirkinjeh who own the soil . . . " (Murray's Handbook, etc.; I didn't see anything left from this intensive cultivation).—G. S.

AFTERNOON

We walked around as much as we could. Now, after the library of Celsus, we sat down to rest a bit. The agora, and the stoa extending far out, before me. To the left the sun setting toward Mount Coressus (Bülbül Daği). On the right, where the drum of a fallen column rests on the ground, a sheaf of cyclamen. Many cyclamen this time in Ephesus constantly remind you of the tones of the Ionian sky. The sweetest body of the day, a living body; the dance of mountain and stone exists here too, a little more tangible than in Attica. At the edge of the stoa I'm looking at, small trees; the guard called them "karaağaç" [elms] . Patches of shade and patches of sun. Suddenly a single hoot of an owl; the time is three in the afternoon.

The drowned harbor of Ephesus has haunted me since morning. It didn't leave me either at the theater with the raging silversmiths crying out: "Great is Diana of the Ephesians!" (Acts 19.23f.), or at the charming wayside odeon. A harbor sunken into the ground, the mouth of the tomb of a once great city and its dead surrounding plain. This has become for me the conductor of the souls of the vanished harbors of Asia Minor: Ayvalik, Halicarnassus, Skala, Smyrna. The Smyrna of thirty years ago was much closer to ancient Ephesus than today's Izmir. Here, too, you partake of the feast of the dead of your own mother city.

EVENING

At the site of Artemis' temple a few oxen stooping and grazing; a column base. This is all that remains of the shrine that shook the ancient world. You find more marbles from Ephesus—cornerstones, columns, capitals— at the mosque of İsa Bey, a little farther on; intermingling of marbles, like the intermingling of blood.

The sun was setting as we passed the "Gate of Persecution" of Ayasuluk. On the hill a disemboweled contemporary church, then the Church of St. John who saw the Apocalypse on Patmos. In the background to the west rose the curtain of the Selçuk castle, its towers and loopholes like a readymade stage set. The guard showed us a short octagonal column, like an altar; it is, he said, the tomb of the saint.

And every shipmaster, and all the company in ships, and sailors, and as many as trade by sea, stood afar off, And cried when they saw the smoke of her burning, saying, What city is like unto this great city! And they cast dust on their heads, and cried, weeping and wailing, saying, Alas, alas, that great city, wherein were made rich all that had ships in the sea by reason of her costliness! for in one hour is she made desolate. (Revelations 18. 17–19.)

St. John the Divine of Justinian's time became the successor, in almost everything, of Artemis [Diana] of the Ephesians. Pilgrims and laymen, priests and great revenues, legends and superstitions. I wonder what the average lifespan of a religion is. If the "political orthodoxies" born in our time last as long as their predecessors, we are not doing remarkably well. So at least thinks a contemporary, an idolator, with regard to them. For the moment, there is consolation in the twilight on the slopes of Ionia, the cyclamen, and the undulation which they still preserve, of the great soul of Heraclitus. These belong to that permanent element that seems to lie behind every religion.

SUNDAY, OCTOBER 22

The despair of the ruins of Asia Minor is indescribable. Everything converges to make it more dismal. The dead, in order to speak, need live blood; that's what is lacking here. Sometimes a stranger passes by, makes the offering of life, and the shade of Teiresias appears or that of Anticleia— then all vanish in boundless silence.

When, yesterday, they guided us through the narrow side corridor of the library ("on the right as you enter") to the sarcophagus of Celsus, the father, I could not help but think of the grave of Lysias the Grammarian.* Shut for a while in the small basement, which the guard was lighting with a kerosene lamp, I could reflect without material distractions upon the

*This is a reference to Cavafy's poem "The Grave of the Grammarian Lysias (42).

harbor of Ephesus in the good years, this gateway of the East. Ships and caravans; an endless coming and going between the coast and the interior; natives, sojourners, sailors, barbarians, mixtures of interests, of religions, of races; Greek learning and Levantinism, eroticism and superstition. I felt little difference between this harbor and the harbors of Smyrna or Alexandria around the end of the nineteenth century. They talk about Cavafy's worship of Hellenism. They must be right, of course. However, if it were only that, he could easily have given us what the Rangavises and so many others gave us. Cavafy never loses touch with his own life; it burns him, and he knows it is exactly the same when he expresses it in the Alexandria of Lathyrus, the Antioch of Julian, or the area of Rue Lepsius. He may change clothes, but beneath the clothes, his voice, his reactions, his gestures remain the same. What makes Cavafy interesting is this give and take of life he maintains with the world of the past.

We were shut in from morning until dark; a population census. The seafront deserted, except for two or three passersby now and then—the censors. The difference from the daily routine is not great. Izmir is the most lifeless city I have ever seen; it is constantly carrying on a census.

At nightfall old Agathovoulos arrived with a middle-aged friend of his, a doctor of mixed nationality. We went out to a shop for loukoumades [fried dough puffs]. The old tradition of making loukoumades has not been lost, like the tradition of the Greek waterfront language, which remains the lingua franca of Smyrna. The doctor told us this story:

"They called me in to see a sick woman in a house near Parallel Street. I went up to the bedroom. The sick woman (it was nothing, just a stomachache) was lying on the floor, at the foot of the bed which was made up and decorated. I stayed for a moment in the room downstairs and noticed a faucet stuck into the wall among pictures and photographs. 'What's this?' I asked the landlord. 'See how lucky I am!' he replied. 'The other day the children were playing. Their game was to hammer nails in the wall. As they were hammering a nail in, water suddenly gushed out. I called a tinsmith at once, and he screwed in this faucet. And now I don't have to carry water from outside.' "

MONDAY, OCTOBER 23

In the morning to the museum. It is housed in the Church of St. Vouklos, the only church of ours still standing. The beautiful, carved, wooden double door with St. George and St. Demetrius, which I saw in the women's section, certainly doesn't belong to it. At the entrance clay sarcophagi; they remind me strongly of the one we found in our vineyard; perhaps it was one of them. But the only thing I saw with Vourla inscribed as its place of origin was a mosaic representing a horseman with his hound. I recalled statues of young women with hairdos like those in photographs of my grandmother's time, a golden laurel crown, small terracotta maenads with sensitive breasts, and also this: a big statue of Maeander from Ephesus—the name Cayster would suit it well. The river god reclining, as at banquets, holding up the horn of Amalthea filled with various fruits: pine cones, quinces, apples, citrons, lemons, and grapes. The head with its luxuriant hair is crowned with flowers. The moustache drooping around the mouth and the beard bring to mind something of Christ's face. This marble does not represent anything noteworthy. However, it held me and I looked at it for some time. Its mediocre art made it both exist and not exist; its body did not invite you to touch it; the fruits it offered were of stone; a melancholy thing; if it had been lost, it wouldn't have mattered. It gazed into the distance as if to say that it cared not a bit that all had turned to dust.

At noon we ate at Boutza. We stayed until evening. We walked around outside before it grew dark. Here everything is left as it was, and rotting. The once wealthy summer resort has become a lake of desolation, where empty villas are marooned, hollow and frail. Suddenly children's songs in an enclosed courtyard. Breath. Then it is worse.

Oh, to save myself from this writhing of death pursuing me for so many days!

Now it is common to speak about the catastrophe of war. However, something that weighs heavier in your guts is the sudden extermination of a fully alive world, with its lights, with its shadows, with its rituals of joy and sorrow, with the tightly woven net of its life. To hear still

in your ears the cracking of its joints at the hour of its extinction.
And the ugly caprices of that hour. This destiny in your blood that has
merged at last, inevitably, with the destiny of the contemporary world
horror is a different matter. The theater of Hierapolis, the theater of Stratoniceia, the theater of Pergamum, the theater of Ephesus—you used to
try to imagine the rows of eyes in these theaters, how they watched.
You contemplate them now as it grows dark and they seem like seashells
in the hands of children. In this theater you watched a tragedy that had
no end, for it was not allowed to find its catharsis. The sun is setting over
the Two Brothers; twilight spreads across sky and sea, the color of an
inexhaustible love. And you are ashamed that you want to howl that it
is an enormous lie. Because you know that the circle has not closed, that
the Furies set loose in this confined and distant place upon the great and
the small of the earth are not sleeping, and neither you nor your children
will see them "in the depths of the earth."*

TUESDAY, OCTOBER 24

S.S. ISKENDERUN, UNDER WAY

In the morning we walked around the old marketplace, passed by the
bazaar, and embarked at about two for Constantinople. On the ship
people as thick as ants: visitors admiring the new acquisition of the state
shipping line.

We now follow the course the little steamer used to take when it carried
us to Skala. We called it The Constantine (Captain Kirkor, an awful
drunk). Smyrna, as we sail away, seems endless. For me it is no more
populous than the gorge of Korama.†

The fortress seems like a hill you could hold in your hand; how memory
magnifies the size; only the mountains keep their normal size. I easily
make out the cartroad of Vourla. We are going much faster than in other

*Aeschylus, Eumenides, l. 1036.
†See Tris Imeres sta Monastiria tis Kappadokias (Athens, 1953).—G. S.

times; already St. John's Island. The first time I've seen Skala from this angle. As we turn toward Phokies, this bay surrounded by islands takes on the appearance of a sanctuary forbidden to man. But again and again this instinct of the earth; unimaginable how it expands within you— this roaring of blood or sap; we must have been trees in the beginning. Faces that shone, tender lips that laughed, voices; I'm writing with my brother's pen. God, have mercy upon our dead! Such air, such tones, such warmth, such light—they don't let you break away from them; they hold you, delay you longer and longer—this sensation of a bare autumn resurrection. My eyes, I think, are full; they have room for nothing else.

We went down to the small lounge. About twenty passengers sit and talk, their eyes staring fixedly into the void, just as when you wait in the barbershop.

Ionia, a great princess' perfect diadem thrown into a drawer of old newspapers filled with such vituperations no one understands any more. The moral of this whole story may be, for the people, the remark my diplomat companion made last July: "The Greeks say the Turks burned Smyrna; the Turks say the Greeks burned it. Who can tell which is the truth?"

The evil has been committed; the significant question is who will redeem the evil.

We passed Mytilene as it was growing dark. In the direction of the moon, a full moon, the dark shores: Pergamum, Ayvalik: not a soul, only the eye of God. I've learned by now the quality of desolation in these lands. In the direction the sun had set you spell out the lights of the island and see the little boats setting out for fishing or poaching.

WEDNESDAY, OCTOBER 25

We draw near Istanbul to the sound of amanades (not that such things do not happen in our country). The ship's loudspeakers are nerve-

wracking; such a beautiful ship. The sea is leaden; the land on shore dull
white. The minarets like reeds; and Hagia Sophia. In the evening we take
the train for Ankara.

MONDAY, OCTOBER 30. ANKARA

Yesterday the Turkish national holiday; formalities, etc. General decoration with flags, everything drowned in red. We returned on St. Demetrius'
Day. Here is another sun, a dry one; letters waiting, and the boredom,
now customary, of lagging uncertainty, and of the environment. You
answer, just as you gesticulate, out of habit; not that you expect anything
from your writing.

"And he gathered all the book peddlers, and some had books that came
from the palace of the books which the Christians Roum burned, when
Amrou ben El-Ash entered El-Iskederia" (Arabian Nights, Mardrus, VI,
431).

And yet
beneath God's step
the cyclamen bend.

SATURDAY, NOVEMBER 4

They relate the following brief exchange at Constantinople. Someone asks
Mr. Platypodas (who carries on the tradition of the old Swiss mercenaries):
"Will you see St. Sophia?" Answer: "One can live without seeing St.
Sophia."

Another: Someone expresses his antipathy for the Frankish Crusaders of
1204. And he, almost reproachfully: "And yet, if the Franks had stayed,
we wouldn't have bedbugs in Greece." You feel like shouting: Long live
the bedbugs!

This reminds me of London in the old days, that doctor, a raving anti-
Venizelian, who shouted: "Venizelos is a traitor because he built drainage

works in Macedonia; mosquitoes, malaria, and typhoid, Gentlemen, are the natural weapons of the Greeks."

Will there ever come a time in Greece when such talk will seem incredible?

MONDAY, NOVEMBER 6

I woke at dawn's haziest hour and glanced at the street; endless silence and fog. On the square bank building opposite, the flag, forgotten since yesterday, was waving lazily; this was the only motion. Intense impression that I saw the world like a landscape of nothingness.

WEDNESDAY, NOVEMBER 8

Extreme emotion when I think about the renaissance of the Palaeologoi. This more intensely since last September when I started working again on the Travelogue on Cappadocia.

Returning from Smyrna, I tried to approach a poem. As always here the gift of God is drowned in a pool of torpor. Furthermore, I need quadruple effort to do anything. Never before have I needed such will to write the twenty-five pages of Cappadocia—not even when I wrote the essay on Erotokritos, which had nonetheless plunged me into indescribable despair. No one can realize what difficult conditions I work under and how dearly I pay for my profession. But what profession in Greece would I not pay more dearly for? And the literary marketplace of Athens?

TUESDAY, NOVEMBER 21

For ten months now, Angelos has been buried under foreign soil.

I have felt his loss more heavily since my last trip. His letters: "As you say, America is a dreadful place. Shangri-la. You live—die, you don't even know it yourself. This place is a hill with tall, very tall pine trees (they bear no resemblance to those of Attica), bare and bushy at the top, like those on Chinese vases. And all kinds of exotic birds; they fly differently, have different colors. The partridges, insolent, come and untie your shoelaces. Below the hill (about half an hour) the city of Monterey, where California's independence was declared a hundred years ago . . . What do I want, how have I been cast ashore here?" (his unfinished letter to me from the Monterey Presidio, Sunday evening, September 11, 1949). I laughed about the partridges: his perpetual humor, even in difficult hours.

Neohellenic whimsies: "I went to Washington . . . result: zero. I have no doubt whatsoever that the nonexistent Greek Information Office, which does not exist except to give groundless information, must have said again that I am a 'communist.' They spread the matter around so systematically and so stubbornly that they have almost convinced the communists themselves." Our unlucky country.

The feeling of New York: "This country is starving spiritually amid her gold, like Midas. All this is relative of course . . . There's no place where you see man's naked soul more than over here; blacks with bloody faces, women crying in the subway (the 'hypodrome,' as I call it*); no one even turns to look . . . Indifference or fear? Both" (from New York to me, January 16, 1948).

These are gone, if they are gone. But the live thing burning me is that the typed pages of his poems have been lost. The verses of his that I found have such a personal vibration. Angelos has an eye, and often his expression spans very wide vistas or dimensions.

SATURDAY, NOVEMBER 25

Yesterday the Comédie-Française, some good, some bad—as the Comédie-Française usually is. In the afternoon a speech by the mature leading lady, illustrated with recitation of texts. A sign of the times or the places: much more prose than poetry. The talk began with the seventeenth century and ended with Péguy; after 1914, silence. The occasion caused a ripple on the surface of Ankara; French as I knew it in my youth, not

*The word "hypodrome" (under path) is evidently a play on the word hippodrome.

as it is spoken now in diplomatic circles. As that French learning sprang to
the surface, it looked to me like the anachronistic appearance of Greek in
the years of Ptolemy Lathyrus or Gregory of Nazianzus.

In the evening at dinner, as I was talking with two young supporting
actresses, one of them said: "When I'm around fifty-five, I can hope to be
a good tragic actress." I was impressed by this remark in a time when we
have become accustomed to seeing the young always in a hurry. This
young girl reckoned that she had twenty-five years of hard work before
her. The work of the past day is added to the work of the day to follow:
I like this tempo. Not for one man only but also for the generations
after him. During my student years in Paris I once visited with a friend
the apartment of a bow maker (for violins). It was on the top floor of a
house in the vicinity of the Gare du Nord. To the right, as I entered,
an orderly pile of unplaned wood. "All this," I asked, "will you make it
into bows?" "Not I," he replied, "it will be made into bows by my son;
the wood has not dried yet." I was impressed by this consciousness of
continuity. How many know to wait for the wood to dry.

MONDAY, DECEMBER 11

A dream: the other was expressing himself as he usually does, but he was
at the same time me. Notice in dreams this undulation or fluidity of
the ego: when you do not know whether or not the self of the other
expresses your own self too.

Works that are good because they please, and those that are good, regardless of whether they please or not; mark this distinction.

I met Louis MacNeice; he read poems from Yeats down to his own generation, in a small packed room at the University; except for a few men, all
young girls. I was impressed with the way his recitation changed, when at
the end he read three of his own poems: another tone, warmer, at times
carried away with himself. I wouldn't say, as one might think, that he
didn't care for the other poets; I suspect that, since he's such a shy man,
he had to gather more momentum to present his own self.

SUNDAY, DECEMBER 17, CONSTANTINOPLE

We left Ankara (vacation) yesterday for Athens; we are taking the boat on the 23rd. If I don't go in person to see what is to become of me they'll make me cool my heels forever. We went down to the konak (the old Tokatlian). Our window faces the courtyard of the Armenian church. Two pigeons came to sleep in the gutter opposite; motionless like a bas-relief on a Byzantine parapet.

1951

JANUARY, KIFISSIA

Now I Joseph was walking, and I walked not. And I looked up to the air and saw the air in amazement. And I looked up unto the pole of the heaven and saw it standing still, and the fowls of the heaven without motion. And I looked upon the earth and saw a dish set, and workmen lying by it and their hands were in the dish: and they that were chewing chewed not, and they that were lifting the foot lifted it not, and they that put it to their mouth put it not thereto, but the faces of all of them were looking upward. And behold there were sheep being driven, and they went not forward but stood still; and the shepherd lifted his hand to smite them with his staff, and his hand remained up. And I looked upon the stream of the river and saw the mouths of the kinds upon the water and they drank not. And of a sudden all things moved onward in their course. (Protevangelium of James, 18.2)*

MONDAY, JANUARY 24. XENIA MELATHRON

We came to stay in Athens. For how long?

A blind man playing his harmonica before the formidable wall (the side wall) of the National Library.

Last Sunday, for the first time, to the Amphiareion.

I read from one inscription:

Ο ΔΗΜΟΣ ΩΡΩΠΙΩΝ
ΤΙΜΑΡΧΟΝ ΘΕΟΔΩΡΟΥ
ΑΡΕΤΗΣ ΕΝΕΚΕΝ†

I do not know this Timarchos, nor his virtue. Never mind, they felt the need to mention it.

The "beauty" or the translucency, o altra cosa, of Attica is so potent—in the medical sense, I mean—that you must adjust your senses in order to absorb it in small doses; otherwise it maddens or stupifies you.

WEDNESDAY

Last week with Gelon at Sikelianos'. The nobility he had during his struggle with death three years ago has left. Now he doesn't even go out; one of his legs won't respond. We found him in bed. By I don't know what inspiration of the traffic authorities, his street, so quiet in other days, has become one of the noisiest in Athens. But as always he doesn't

---

*The Apocryphal New Testament, translated by Montague Rhodes James (Oxford, 1953), p. 46.
†The People of the Oropians / to Timarchos, Son of Theodoros, / on Account of His Virtue.

complain about a thing. Unfortunately, as it seems, it's difficult to find him alone. Even this evening a certain gloomy writer happened to be there; it wasn't easy to relieve the atmosphere. He told a couple of jokes, however, that fell flat. The mood was unbearably depressing. Now as I write I'm thinking about his image: death, snowing upon him, has covered him half way.

SUNDAY, FEBRUARY 11

Myloi near Anapli [Nauplion]; at Kephalari; the church of Zoodochos Pege carved within the rock. The landscape below brings to mind very clearly the painting by Makriyannis and Panayiotis Zographos.

Oranges of Eurotas; oranges everywhere—their color startling, alien to any idea you had about Sparta. So much, that in the evening at the restaurant I felt somewhat stupid listening to the young waiter answering: "I am a Spartan."

Wide streets. Sparta makes you think of a child wearing his father's jacket. The hotel is called the Menelaion; at night its walls sweat snores. When I turned off the light Myloi near Anapli had totally merged with Makriyannis' painting.

MONDAY

Since morning at Mistra; all stones and mullein; that yellow-green color.

Apricots of Korama, blackberries of Matiana, mullein of Mistra; Greece, Greece—my God!

This, too, is a sacred landscape.

The Pantanassa, a nunnery; eight nuns, they told us. The abbess welcomed us; a neat, tidy hall; flowers in the vases, carpets. I was moved by the frescoes: Palm Sunday, the Resurrection of Lazarus.

At noon we ate near the Palace. Four or five children had been following us since the morning. When from time to time you ask them about their parents, they answer, "my father was killed by the rebels." Horrible how many orphans there are here. I persuade one of these little ones to tell us a fairy tale; he speaks of a king in the same way he recites his lesson; the spell of the fairy tale seems to have been lost even at this age: "he put on the cloak and turned into wind" (i.e., he vanished), he said.

Manolis Triandaphyllidis, who is with us, mentions a beautiful expression I'd never heard: "the shadows have begun," when the shadows spread at sunset.

TUESDAY

In the morning to the few ancient ruins that still remain. The landscape of the Lacedaemonians is absolutely idyllic; perhaps this is fate's way of punishing their obstinacy.

Nevertheless, the nobility of Taygetos is spellbinding.

It was growing dark as we entered Anapli. The sea a pond; Bourtzi just a bas-relief. Enclosed courtyards with huge growths of algae. The oil lamp is always burning at the Prime Minister's assassination.* At the harbor in a window, a woman combing her hair. Bodies of lovers. Why do I enjoy the patina of this small city? The same, one night with Tonio on Syros. A feeling I miss in Athens.

WEDNESDAY

Asine is so close; we didn't go; better this way. Meal at Megalo Pefko. The last time, before Ankara, I was here with Sikelianos. When he leaves us, there will be much desolation. Raw desolation.

*Ioannis Kapodistrias (1776–1831), President of the Greek republic, was assassinated on October 9, 1831, as he was entering the church.

SUNDAY, FEBRUARY 18

The <u>honest</u> Elpenor: Each day the Athenians make him pay a fine so he'll stop being honest. Each morning he vows to behave himself, but he starts all over again.

This is striking(?): the present-day(?) hatred of the Greeks—not the obvious, but the latent, innate; everybody against everybody else.

FRIDAY, FEBRUARY 23

Walking toward Kydathenaion Street, in a cramped lot near Amalias Avenue, riderless, wooden ponies, going round and round while the hand-organ whined. The instantaneous feeling that this is the picture of our country's political life.

A glance at the Acropolis:

Marbles
neither standing nor leaving
in great despair.

WEDNESDAY, FEBRUARY 28

Opening the window in the morning, the <u>light</u>. And right afterward a black curtain: the people I'm going to meet all day—who prevent me from seeing my land.

THURSDAY, MARCH 1

On April 15th I must be in London. Eight months lost—heaven knows why.

Mrs. Daphnopatis says that when she once met Bernard Shaw and asked him how the Acropolis impressed him, he replied: "Like a folded umbrella." Should one conclude perhaps that G.B.S. did not have the ability to see anything outside of the United Kingdom—or possibly Mrs. Daphno-patis got on his nerves?

MARCH 12, CLEAN MONDAY. S.S. SAMSUN

I'm leaving to wind up Turkey. Maró will be waiting for me to pick her up at Piraeus. Utterly exhausted, I went to bed right away, resolved not to get up until evening. I remained in Greece over two and a half months; I didn't expect this stay to be so long. I'm leaving contaminated with the sin of despair: the people, an illness (don't even mention the political world and the Administration!); they prevent you from seeing and they spoil whatever you see; others are made of cotton dipped in a neurotic haze. I lasted as long as I could; I don't know what I paid for this endurance with.

However, lying down, as soon as I heard the engines' throbbing, I dressed again and went above; I couldn't resist. You look at the mountains, the houses at their feet, and the people along the Piraeus waterfront crowding like ants to the Koulouma,* and you say: My God, forgive us for thinking about this swamp we have been condemned to.

At about 18:00 we were past Sounion; such a light; the cliff with the temple behind it golden, a patch of dark blue hillside, farther to the right the rose-colored tones of the rock fading into the dark sea. Behind me, to the west, the mountain of Aegina and the other mountains half-faded but strikingly present: "and I looked up unto the pole of the heaven and saw it standing still." These mountains, as the colored wings touch them, draw you to a place where you cannot help being a visionary. But here's the horror: the attraction and the distance from men. How can these things be made tangible?

We started out with the paper streamers from yesterday's carnival festivi-ties. As we leave the harbor an old peasant woman asks me: "Where's the third class? I left my son behind; I cried a lot and I lose my way."

*Koulouma, the festivities on Clean Monday, first day of Great Lent. It is cele-brated throughout Greece with excursions to the countryside, lenten meals, dancing, and kite-flying.

Tears have become kites.

Perhaps these tears redeem us.

TUESDAY

We arrived at Constantinople in early afternoon; chores. Nevertheless, before the light vanished, I broke away and went to the Monastery of Stoudion. Roofs and minarets delineated in the light mist. The dream of Constantinople was dancing tremulously. It was growing dark in the courtyard of the ruined monastery. A softness. It's good for the last encounter to be like this. I'll spend the night on the train.

WEDNESDAY. ON THE TRAIN TO ANKARA

As I'm drinking my morning tea in the coach, a Jewish merchant says to a foreign co-traveler, pointing to the landscape of Ankara: "Regardez, les chèvres d'Ankara brillent au soleil."

For a moment I wonder if I will miss the protection of the Anatolian steppe.

FRIDAY, MARCH 30. S.S. ANKARA

My last days in Turkey burned out amid crates, formalities, and hand-shakes and, at the last moment, last Wednesday, a telegraph that M. was suddenly operated on Monday (appendicitis); the timetables must change; I'll stay two weeks in Athens again. I said goodbye to Constantinople at noon, not without sadness; I hadn't seen as much of it as I wanted to.

MONDAY, APRIL 16

We set out from Piraeus on Saturday by the same boat that brought me from Constantinople. M. made a rapid and good recovery. Yesterday, out in the open sea, two swallows, off course, came aboard the boat.

At 14:00 p.m. we disembarked at Naples. Mediterranean cities with the old gentleness, rude insults, and clothes drying in the narrow streets; often great poverty, men in incredible rags. Physiognomies as though carved out of wood or copied from marionettes of the puppet theater. Old men and women, such as I haven't seen for many years, haunted; old women with veils and hats of other times, pre-Mussolinian or Pirandellian; one holding a bunch of white violets, half-withered; another unbelievably wrinkled, but still upright, heavily made up. Somewhere, in corners, your eye grasps spectacles of harsh, sanctified realism: a crucifix behind a curtain, a horribly painted semblance of the massacred human body.

We were able to visit the museum for an hour; I didn't ask to see anything but the frescoes of Pompeii. The mosaics, a permanent impression.

We drank beer at a small harbor with boats and yachts. Half-naked young men; "touristic" sexualism, the kind that pleases American women; general lasciviousness in the eyes of the young men; I didn't chance to see one beautiful woman. You live among these people and you think of the dictator, that ogre who dealt out blows to the head. A Neapolitan sunset; such colors. In this respect Constantinople is remarkably superior and nobler.

TUESDAY

This morning waking up, dolphins; then seagulls; toward sundown, spring fragrances from the shores of Corsica. We passed the northern cape of the island around 19:00. In the morning we will be at Marseilles. The first time I've felt like myself in months; a breathing spell.

WEDNESDAY

We will start out at 23:00 for Paris—Calais. There's no time for dawdling. France looks like the France I knew, just as a stage set looks like a familiar landscape. What's missing? We went to wash up and leave our luggage in a room of the Grand Hôtel; a room facing the courtyard; it even has a fireplace; a very familiar part of the earth; the boredom of old student rooms is glued to the wallpaper, the curtains; inevitably one breathes pages of Marcel Proust.

We went out. People much better fed than the Neapolitans. We climbed up to Notre Dame de la Garde by the funicula. A different light, dull. We went for bouillabaisse at a restaurant recommended to us. When we went in we were the only customers. As we were waiting for the fish soup, the restaurant began filling up; men, women, children, and an amazingly heavy baby. All with gluttony culminating in their jaws, robust jaws. They served us ceremoniously. I asked what kind of fish they used. "Ce sont des poissons propices à la bouillabaisse," said the waiter. Scorpion (the fish) is called "rascasse," but I like the word "propice" at that hour of sacred rite. It must be more than ten years since I've seen such a feast. The smoke thickened, the colors gleamed, colors from lobsters, fish, vegetables, flames from spirit lamps. These people were devouring astonishing quantities with teeth, with nostrils, with eyes. I felt a frightening crescendo welling up; the act of eating took on the same frenzied meaning that the act of dancing must once have had for primitive races. I felt out of breath. Finally the idea came to me that the fixed thought motivating all these eaters, as they were cleaning their dishes, was the thought of a definitive assimilation, an ultimate conquest, and a looming threat—"encore un repas que l'ennemi ne mangera pas," as they used to say in other times.

Just as I was paying, the proprietor came over and said [in English] : "Have you enjoyed your lunch?" I replied that I was neither an American nor an Englishman but a Mediterranean. Embarrassed that he hadn't psychologized the customer correctly, he repeated, "Àvez-vous bien mangé, Monsieur?" I said we were going to England. And he: "Il paraît que l'on se serre la ceinture là-bas. On se l'est bien serrée, nous autres aussi."

The ease of France can dissolve you. England, I don't know. But Greece cannot, as long as you calculate your distances, which is difficult.

THURSDAY, APRIL 19

We arrived at Paris at 9:00. Two hours at our disposal; we went out and walked around. It was drizzling.

Puis rien ne saurait faire
Que mon spleen ne chemine
Sous les spleens insulaires
Des petites pluies fines . . .*

We passed the Pont d'Austerlitz. Ile Saint Louis. We entered Nôtre Dame. The great rose windows were lighted properly by the gloomy day; then, suddenly, the organ. I thought of the people praying in this church when Paris was falling. I had heard its litany from the radio at Kydathenaion Street. Those tragic death throes of France. We took a taxi: Boulevard Saint Michel, Luxembourg, and back to Gare de Lyon. There was something haunting about this tour. The train crosses Paris for some time: leprous houses, railroad landscapes, sad clothes drying at the windows in endless drizzle: "Gare de la douleur" how many times. My God, let me grow old and die in my homeland!

We've left Paris. The weather always overcast; hoarfrost surrounding the trees; mistletoe. Our co-travelers kill the time with illustrated magazines; no one lifts his head. I am surprised; I had forgotten that we were entering countries where people don't look at the outside world.

*Jules Laforgue, Oeuvres complètes (Paris, 1947), II, 64.